Ordering Information:

Quantity sales. Special discounts are available on quantity purchases by corporations, associations, and others.

Affiliates. Affiliate and network marketing opportunities are available for this book.

* * *

Contact Information:

Christopher Penn at cspenn@trustinsights.ai or on the contact page on www.TrustInsights.ai

Written and Published in the United States of America.

AI For Marketers

An Introduction and Primer - Third Edition

Christopher S. Penn

Preface to the Third Edition

The first edition of this book sprang to life largely due to the insistence of Ann Handley, Chief Content Officer of MarketingProfs. Back in 2017, she asked for a simple guide, a set of blog posts, that would help her understand what all the hubbub about artificial intelligence was. I wrote a series of 9 posts on the topic, and when the series was done, I bundled them up into an eBook, added some more examples, and called that AI for Marketers.

The first edition did its job of providing some of the basics and practical applications of AI for marketing purposes, but by no means was it a proper book. In fact, for those of you who purchased it, you can still see artifacts in the text from its blog lineage.

But it was woefully incomplete. In 2019, I rewrote it from the ground up, and the Second Edition was born. More complete. More accurate. More thorough.

In the two years since, I've presented the contents of the book on stage hundreds of

times, and fielding thousands of questions about the application of AI in marketing. Those questions, along with the breakneck pace of innovation in the field, are what has led to the Third Edition. To be honest, two years between editions is probably too long, but for whatever reason at the end of 2019, I didn't feel like a Third Edition was right for the time.

It is now. So much has changed since 2019, from groundbreaking new models and technologies to shocking and frightening abuses of the technology. We have so much more to learn and explore together, so thank you for being here for this Third Edition.

Table of Contents

Why is AI in Marketing Important?

What does every CMO, every CEO, every Board of Director ask of us, ask of marketing?

Better.
Faster.
Cheaper.

These are timeless demands.

Make marketing more effective and impactful.
Make marketing reach the customer and help close the sale sooner.
Make marketing cost less.

How are we doing, as a profession?

Instead of **better**, arguably marketing's quality is worsening. Why? We're faced with more data than ever. In 2020, as a species, IDC and Seagate estimated[1] that humans generated about 50 zettabytes of data.

A zettabyte is an unimaginably large number. It's the same amount of space on a billion laptop computers. Here's an easy way to think about a zettabyte. The average show on Netflix takes up about 1 gigabyte of data for an hour's entertainment. If you were to embark on the most ambitious binge-watching ever, and you started in the Eocene era, 55 million years ago, with no breaks, you'd just be getting to the end of your first zettabyte now. If you were to attempt to watch 50 zettabytes of data? You're talking about starting a billion years before the Earth itself existed, 5.7 billion years ago.

Facebook alone, according to Visual Capitalist and Raconteur,[2] generated 4 petabytes of data per day in 2020. A petabyte, as a reminder, is 1,000 terabytes. That fancy new laptop you just bought? A petabyte would be the disk space of 1,000 of those. Can you imagine filling 1,000 laptops a day of data?

Can you imagine trying to analyze the data on those laptops, as a marketer? Whether we like Facebook or not, that's still an insane amount of data that people create every day - and that's just one platform.

* * *

Even something like traditional news - which has suffered mightily in the last couple of

---

[1] https://www.seagate.com/files/www-content/our-story/trends/files/idc-seagate-dataage-whitepaper.pdf

years - still churns out around 200,000 news stories per day. That's 139 news stories per second. Imagine trying to be heard, trying to stand out, when faced with a firehose of news that big.

Data volume isn't the only problem we face as marketers. We've got a pretty serious data quality problem, too. How many of us have this email address and its many variations in our CRM systems?

test@test.com

I'd be surprised if you didn't have that in your database. We have a massive data quality problem in marketing, and that's a major reason why marketing isn't better.

How big is this problem?

According to the January 2020 CMO Survey,[3] when 500 CMOs were asked what percentage of time analytics were used in making decisions, respondents answered a shockingly low **37.7% of the time**.

---

[2] https://www.visualcapitalist.com/wp-content/uploads/2019/04/data-generated-each-day-full.html

Take a moment to think about that. 37.7% is just slightly more than one in three. So, put another way, roughly two-thirds of CMOs do NOT use analytics for decision making.

What are they using instead? Experience? "Gut instinct"? Wild guessing? Some combination of the three?

It's no wonder marketing has a quality problem, and no wonder why we are greeted with skepticism when we ask for more budget, more resources, more capabilities. We simply can't show that what we're doing is working, or that we're learning and adapting from our mistakes.

So, better's out. What about **faster**? Is our marketing faster? Are we helping our businesses reach audiences faster, engaging prospects faster, closing sales faster?

The speed at which data is flying at us isn't slowing down. Quite the opposite: data is coming at us faster than ever before - and not just us, but our audiences as well. In a single

---

[3] https://cmosurvey.org

day in 2021, it's estimated we'll generate 320 billion emails, or 3.7 million emails per second.

Per. Second.

Want a visual of that? Imagine one email was a leaf on a tree. The average large oak or maple tree contains about a quarter million leaves. Now, imagine 15 large trees dropping all their leaves on you at once, every second. That's what 3.7 million emails per second might look like.

Consumers are also spending more, faster online. It's trite to say it, but the last year truly has been unprecedented in living memory. A pandemic that forced everyone indoors for a substantial part of the year also exploded data creation. Broadband analytics firm OpenVault projected[4] monthly household usage of 500 GB per month in North America, an increase of 47% year over year.

Were you prepared? Was your data infrastructure prepared?

Consider how much data is involved in each sale, in each interaction, in each touchpoint with the customer. Now consider how human most marketing departments are. At one company I worked at in the past, there were dozens of 20-somethings manually Googling for news stories of the day, trying to keep up with the tsunami emerging from the firehose. No human team - no dozens, not hundreds, not even thousands of people - can keep up with the scale and speed of marketing data we're generating today.

It's no wonder our marketing isn't getting faster.

Better's not working for us, and neither is faster. At least we're getting more cost-efficient, right?

Well... no. Marketing is **not getting cheaper**.

According to the same CMO Survey, marketing spending reached all-time highs in 2020, accounting or 12.6% of the overall company budget and 11.4% of company revenues. The spending patterns in 2020 were focused - unsurprisingly - heavily on digital, with 8.4% growth in digital spending year over year,

---

[4] https://openvault.com/whats-ahead-in-2021-well-hazard-a-guess/

5.7% growth in CRM investments, 2.1% in brand spending. The only area which declined in 2020 was traditional (non-digital) ad spend, which declined 5.3%.

Marketing is spending, spending, spending. Yet, are CMOs getting what they paid for? Since August of 2017, CMOs have rated marketing ROI as flat, while other key financial metrics such as sales revenues and profits have increased in the same time frame.

So, to summarize:

Marketing ***isn't getting better***, overwhelmed by data quality and quantity issues.

Marketing ***isn't getting faster*** than the consumer's data, but slower.

Marketing ***isn't getting cheaper***, lagging behind other key financial metrics.

What's the impact of this failure to achieve our core goals?

Budget cuts.

Staff reductions.

* * *

Increasingly unrealistic demands not based in any kind of data.

How do we prevent these outcomes? We have to find our way to better, faster, and cheaper - and quickly. More important, we have to do so nimbly; the world changed more in 2020 than at any time in living memory, and the pace of change continues to accelerate. Whatever solution we find to becoming better, faster, and cheaper must also permit us to pivot quickly when circumstances change.

What solution could do this?

The answer, unsurprisingly, is artificial intelligence.

Artificial intelligence promises three things - if we implement it well - the three As:

Acceleration: reaching results faster than with human or traditional computing processes.

Accuracy: reaching better results than with human or traditional computing processes, especially with very large datasets.

* * *

Automation: reducing repetitive, low-value work for humans, freeing us up to do more valuable, better-suited tasks.

Does this sound familiar? It should. **AI, when implemented correctly, promises faster, better, and cheaper**.

Consider the companies that have mastered the use of AI. What are they capable of offering?

- Tech giants such as Google and Facebook provide incredible services to billions of people at comparatively low costs - including free, the ultimate cheap.
- Major consumer companies like Target and Walmart provide goods of high quality – especially compared to just two decades ago – at lower prices than ever, whenever we want it.
- Is there anyone who isn't familiar with Amazon and its endless quest to provide goods and services to us as quickly as possible?

These companies have made AI a strategic priority and have rolled it out in production, at scale, to achieve better, faster, and cheaper. None of these gigantic firms could maintain their competitive[5] advantages without the extensive use of artificial intelligence. We might not think of traditional companies like Walmart as AI leaders, but a quick look at sites like Google Scholar and arXiv.org show dozens of academic papers published by employees at these firms around the use of AI.

* * *

Anomaly Detection for an E-commerce Pricing System

Jagdish Ramakrishnan
Walmart Labs
San Bruno, CA
jramakrishnan@walmartlabs.com

Elham Shaabani
Walmart Labs
San Bruno, CA
Elham.Shaabani@walmartlabs.com

Chao Li
Walmart Labs
San Bruno, CA
CLI0@walmart.com

Mátyás A. Sustik
Walmart Labs
San Bruno, CA
MSustik@walmartlabs.com

ABSTRACT

Online retailers execute a very large number of pr... updates when compared to brick-and-mortar stores. Even a few mi...priced items can have a significant ... ... tomer trust. Early detec... ... ... fashion is an importan... per, we describe unsup... approaches we develo... pricing system at Wal... in batch and real-time... are reviewed and actio... We found that having... to facilitate model perf... speed were important factors influencing model selection, parameter choice, and prioritization in a production environment for a large-scale system. We conducted analyses on the performance of various approaches on a test set using real-world retail data and fully deployed our approach into production. We found that our approach was able to detect the most important anomalies with high precision.

1 INTRODUCTION

Pricing plays a critical role in every consumer's purchase decision. With the rapid evolution of e-commerce and a growing need to offer consumers a seamless omni-channel (e.g., store and online) experience, it is becoming increasingly important to calculate and update prices of merchandise online dynamically to stay ahead of the competition. At Walmart, the online pricing algorithm is responsible for calculating the most suitable price for tens of millions of products on Walmart.com. The algorithm takes both external data, such as competitor prices, and internal data, such as distributor costs, marketplace prices, and Walmart store prices, as inputs to calculate the final price that meets business needs (e.g., top line and bottom line objectives). The calculation is carried out in real-time with large amounts of data, which includes more than tens of millions of item cost data points and marketplace data points per day at Walmart. Many of the data sources are prone to data errors and some of them are out of the company's control. Data errors could lead to incorrect price calculations that can result in profit and revenue losses. For example, an incorrectly entered cost update for an item could drive a corresponding change for the price of the item. Note that an incorrect price of a digitally distributed

product such as a code for a computer game could trigger significant financial losses within minutes without recourse. In addition, incorrect prices could hurt Walmart's EDLP (Every Day Low Price) ... ... legal risk related to ... ... de customer trust. ... ... ect an anomaly if an ... ... ons from its average ... ... uctuations in price ... ... ch results in many ... ... vant to detect price ... ... ect data errors that ... ... udes item attributes ... ... hannels.

To address this challenge, we developed a machine learning-based anomaly detection system that uses both supervised and unsupervised models. We used many features including prices from other channels, binary features, categorical features, and their transformations. We deployed the system into production in both a batch and streaming setting and implemented a review process to generate labeled data in collaboration with an internal operations team. Although the system was built for detecting pricing anomalies, we believe that the insights learned from model training, testing, and tuning, system and architecture design, and prioritization framework are relevant in any application that requires real-time identification and correction of data quality issues for large amounts of data.

Compared to previously published work on anomaly detection, the novel contributions of this paper are:

- **An anomaly detection approach for a large-scale online pricing system** - While there are numerous applications of anomaly detection [34], including intrusion detection, fraud detection, and sensor networks, there are relatively few references on anomaly detection in a retail setting. To the best of our knowledge, this is the first paper documenting methodologies, model performance, and system architecture on anomaly detection for a large scale e-commerce pricing system.
- **Features and transformations for improving model performance** - The choice of features played an important role in model performance. We used a variety of features as inputs to our models, including price-based, binary, categorical,

---

Why Marketing Needs AI

The largest costs in marketing are human-related, from people to make content at scale to running advertising programs. These costs

---

[5] https://arxiv.org/pdf/1902.09566.pdf

scale upwards at a disproportionate rate to impact delivered; adding more marketers scales at best linearly, because humans only have 24 hours in a day and do any one task relatively slowly.

Compare that with the capabilities of machine learning and artificial intelligence. If I have an analysis problem to solve and sufficient cloud computing infrastructure, instead of having one computer work on the problem, I simply "hire" thousands of temporary computers to instantly complete the job. Once done, those computers move onto other tasks. I could never hire thousands of people in a second and lay them off seconds later – but I can with machines.

If all the tasks in marketing were ideally suited for the ways humans work, this solution wouldn't be much of a solution at all. However, the majority of tasks in marketing are highly repetitive, templated tasks. The email campaign we launch this week varies little from the one we launched a week ago. The social media posts we publish today aren't substantially different than yesterday's.

Thus, we have the ideal environment for AI:

highly-repetitive tasks that we can outsource from humans to machines. In outsourcing these tasks, we increase the speed of our marketing by not having to wait for humans to finish their work at human speeds. We spend significantly less money because we spend less time. And, assuming we've trained our software correctly, the quality should be identical or better than what humans create in a rote tasks.

Fast. Cheap. Good.

We can have it all.

Will Marketing Still Need Humans?

For the foreseeable future, we will still need humans. Machines thus far have proven very poor at thinking across domains, at taking ideas from one domain and applying them to another. Machines are also poor at adapting to highly unpredictable situations, so when a black swan occurs – such as the Ice Bucket challenge, for example – we will still require human ingenuity to participate effectively.

Our machines alleviate the non-creative, rote

work as soon as possible, freeing us up to do more of what we're good at. As anyone with a to-do list knows, the list never gets shorter; as machines do more, our lists of what we will do will continue to grow as well.

The sooner marketers adopt machine learning and artificial intelligence, the sooner we'll achieve better, faster, and cheaper in our marketing organizations.

Why Do Marketers Struggle with AI?

The most innovative marketers routinely pick up new things, try them out, and succeed or fail.

- When email became popular in the late 1990s, innovative marketers latched onto it.
- When websites and SEO surged in popularity in the early 2000s, marketers were there.
- When social media picked up in the mid-2000s, marketers cranked out the MySpace pages with reckless abandon.
- When consumers pivoted to mobile devices in the early part of this decade, marketers squeezed messages into tiny screens and apps.

So, given that marketers have a solid track record of adapting to new realities, why are marketers struggling so much to adapt to artificial intelligence and machine learning?

Two Challenges of Artificial Intelligence and Machine Learning

* * *

Marketers face two challenges with AI that they didn't face with most prior new technologies.

First, AI *isn't a consumer technology*. The end recipient of marketing isn't an artificial intelligence; the end consumer - a human being - remains largely the same. People don't change much or substantially in aggregate; the last major behavioral change prior to the pandemic was the adoption of the smartphone by the consumer.

What has changed is that the conduit to the consumer is now powered by machine learning and AI, from social media algorithms to screenless assistants. As a result, marketers face a new intermediary, rather than a new direct channel to the consumer. **AI is the gatekeeper to the eyes and ears of our audience**, in the form of filters, recommendation engines, and algorithms prioritizing some content over others.

The closest analogy to this situation is the advent of SEO in the early 2000s, when marketers needed to understand how SEO worked – and SEO for search engines was radically different than the way consumers searched for things. Early SEO focused on optimizing content for the machine, sometimes to a point of absurdity, making the content less useful for people but favored highly by machines. Jokes like "An SEO expert walks into a bar, pub, tavern, public house, saloon" stemmed from the stilted, awkward writing SEO experts did for search algorithms instead of people.

Consider how often we, as marketers, lament AI-driven algorithms today. Ask any marketer how well their unpaid social media efforts are going, and you'll more often than not hear complaints about the Facebook News Feed algorithm, or the Instagram algorithm, always accompanied by the same dire outlook: marketing on these platforms is going terribly without paying for visibility. Why? The answer, in part, is because the customer of our marketing is a machine - the algorithm - and not the human on the other side of the machine. Meanwhile, as citizens and consumers, we equally lament how easily these technologies can be employed to malicious ends by those savvy bad actors who help disinformation spread - not only causing civic harm, but flooding the algorithms with content that squeezes out our marketing messaging.

Second, AI and its prerequisites are **_deeply entrenched in mathematics and statistics_** – two fields which are not strong points for most marketers. In fact, the fields of machine learning and data science (a pre-requisite to machine learning) are entirely separate, distinct professions from marketing. Creating an artificial intelligence platform for marketing purposes, from scratch, requires entirely different professional knowledge that the vast majority of marketers do not possess.

For example, many AI algorithms require knowledge of subjects like calculus, statistics and probability, and linear algebra - all subjects typically not included in a business major's education.

While marketers need to know what AI is and what it's capable of (and what it's not capable of), asking marketers to take up a brand-new profession in addition to their current profession is unrealistic unless that's already a career goal.

So how should marketers think about AI as it relates to marketing? Consider the analogy of chefs and farmers. Talented chefs take great ingredients and, using the right tools and skills, transform those ingredients into delicious food. Bring a talented chef to a market and they'll point out which fruits and vegetables are just right, which fish is past its prime, which beef is overpriced and which is a steal. There's a good chance an established chef will have a strong network of preferred merchants to buy from, people the chef knows always deliver great quality ingredients.

However, what's the likelihood that the chef is also a farmer, fisher, or hunter as a professional? Almost none. Why? Chefs focus their efforts at being great at cooking, and knowing what ingredients help or hinder their efforts. They may have some sense of what's gone into an ingredient, but they're not the ones to focus on the details of the ingredient's creation. The chef is unlikely to tell the cattle rancher to change the feed's composition, or advise the farmer to add more nitrogen to their soil.

Let's extend this analogy to data science, machine learning, and artificial intelligence. The typical outcome of an artificial intelligence platform is a model that creates insights or makes decisions. The software - and it is just software - plugs into our marketing infrastructure and spits out highly refined products from the raw ingredients - data, algorithms, and analyses. **The machines are the farmers, and we are the chefs.**

Like the chef, the marketer is probably not going to be doing large-scale, production-level data science and machine learning while simultaneously doing marketing. Like the chef should know what a quality ingredient looks like, the marketer should know what great data, algorithms, models, or decisions look like and be able to provide generally corrective feedback to the machine learning and data science professionals within their organization or agencies to improve quality more. The marketer will likely not be building or training the models that artificial intelligence generates.

By the way, beware of the latest crop of professionals who claim to be data scientists after taking a "6-week crash course in artificial intelligence" certificate or training. There's a good chance these individuals may know some of the basics, but compared to professionals who've been doing AI for a while, they won't be very good. As said above, data science, machine learning, and AI are professions. Would you feel comfortable going to someone who proudly showed off their "6-week crash course in dentistry" certificate? Probably not.

The Difference Between Math and People

When we compare math to people, we see the stark difference between AI and other new technologies. When consumers use social media, email, or mobile devices, at the end of the process we are still interacting with another human being. We can transfer our domain knowledge of how people interact from one medium to the next.

When we try to tackle AI, we now switch from people as the end interaction point to machines and mathematics, areas which marketers typically have less experience.

What this means for us is that **we shouldn't feel bad if we're struggling to incorporate AI and its various component technologies into our marketing**. If you've been feeling left behind or out of the loop in all the AI hype, understand that it's not because you've failed as a marketer. You're not a mathematician, statistician, data scientist, or programmer. That's not your profession. To adapt to the new AI landscape, you'll need to hire these people to complement your marketing and domain expertise in humanity.

Now, let's begin our journey into what marketers need to know about machine learning. Just as the beginning chef needs an introduction to ingredients, utensils, and cooking methods, so do marketers need to know the basics of machine learning and AI.

What is Artificial Intelligence?

As mentioned previously, the goal of this book isn't to transform you into a data scientist or machine learning expert. Those are separate professions. The goal of this book is to help you become familiar with the basic concepts and ideas in machine learning and AI so that you can make better decisions and set better strategies as a marketer.

As consumers, we tend to think of AI by its most publicly obvious applications such as smart assistants like Siri, Alexa, and Google Home, or in big headline events like Tesla self-driving cars or IBM Watson beating humans at Jeopardy. While these are flashy examples of the use of AI, they don't help us understand it any better for use in business, especially in marketing.

For example, vendor companies are slapping "AI" labels on nearly every marketing software product on the market. Who's the real deal, and who's faking it? The next few chapters will help you tune your meter for detecting BS.

Before we can begin discussing how artificial

intelligence and machine learning will impact marketing, we have to establish some basic definitions. Artificial intelligence has become so much of a business buzzword that in some ways, it's meaningless without a clear definition. As Professor Dan Ariely of Duke University says, *"AI is like teenage sex: everyone talks about it, nobody really knows how to do it, everyone thinks everyone else is doing it, and so everyone claims they are doing it."*

So, what is AI?

The Formal Definition of AI

According to the Merriam-Webster dictionary, AI is:

1 : a branch of computer science dealing with the simulation of intelligent behavior in computers

2 : the capability of a machine to imitate intelligent human behavior

This is a really broad definition. Any task which falls under intelligent behavior that a machine can simulate is technically artificial intelligence, such as speech recognition, language processing, vision, hearing, sensory perception, reasoning, logic, emotion, etc. This is one of the reasons why every software vendor on the planet is slapping the AI label on their software. The definition is so broad that they can make a truthful claim, even if their software doesn't help us achieve our core goals of better, faster, or cheaper.

Artificial intelligence is also not new. Many of the key concepts, such as computer vision, natural language processing, and neural networks are years, if not decades old. What's changed, and why we hear so much about it now, is that computing power has become ubiquitous and cheap. What was purely academic theory 30 years ago is practical and achievable on your laptop computer today because of the vast increases in computing power available to everyone.

Artificial intelligence is a very big, broad term - so big that it defies easy definition or clear application, much in the same way that human intelligence is an incredibly big, broad term. Let's get more specific; for the purposes of the rest of this book, we'll focus on a subset of artificial intelligence called machine learning.

* * *

So, what's machine learning? According to distinguished computer scientist Dr. Christopher Bishop:

"Machine learning (ML) is the scientific study of algorithms and statistical models that computer systems use to progressively improve their performance on a specific task. Machine learning algorithms build a mathematical model of sample data, known as 'training data', in order to make predictions or decisions without being explicitly programmed to perform the task."

The latter part is a key part of the definition of machine learning and what makes it far more useful to our BS detectors than the blanket umbrella term of AI: **machines that learn to do a task without being explicitly programmed to perform the task.**

For example, a piece of software can be purpose-built to recognize our corporate logo in images. Given any image, it can help us understand whether a picture contains our logo or not. But this software doesn't necessarily need to learn in order to correctly be called artificial intelligence.

* * *

A piece of software which wasn't expressly built to spot our logo, but can see in general, is using machine learning to acquire the skill of spotting our logo. The software's designers and developers may never have seen our logo, or even intended for their software to be used for logo detection, but because it's capable of learning, it can perform the task.

This is what truly separates out machine learning from other kinds of software. In traditional software, we write the code and it spits out data. This is true of every piece of conventional software you use, from your word processor to Angry Birds. The humans write the code, and the code creates data as an output (even if the data is just a red bird flying at a bunch of green pigs on your phone's screen).

In machine learning, we feed data to machine learning software, and it writes its own code as it learns. Starting with a base set of algorithms, machine learning software learns from data and constantly adjusts/ updates itself as new data becomes available. Imagine a word processor that customized itself the more you wrote. Options that you never used would slowly be taken off menu bars; menu items you used constantly would move closer to the top of the menu.

We see this applied in marketing all the time. When using the machine learning functions of software like Google Ads, the software learns what ads of ours work and what don't, and adjusts our budgets and what ads its shows automatically. We don't need to explicitly decide what ads are working and tell the software what to do. It does it for us.

Thus, for our purposes as marketers trying to evaluate whether a vendor can truly help us use AI to achieve better, faster, or cheaper, we should specifically be looking at whether their software is based on machine learning software or not, and how it learns.

Any software that doesn't learn is not machine learning software by definition and thus cannot be called artificial intelligence.

Before we dive into machine learning, we should spend some time dissecting Dr. Bishop's definition so we better understand the prerequisites of machine learning - understand the ingredients that go into it, so we understand better what we'd need to pursue AI projects of our own.

The Basics of AI: Algorithms and Models

The foundation of artificial intelligence, and of computing itself, begins with the algorithm. As mentioned previously, Dr. Christopher Bishop's definition of machine learning emphasizes algorithms and statistics:

*"Machine learning (ML) is the scientific study of **algorithms** and **statistical models** that computer systems use to progressively improve their performance on a specific task. Machine learning algorithms build a mathematical model of sample data, known as 'training data', in order to make predictions or decisions without being explicitly programmed to perform the task."*

Named after 9th century Persian mathematician Muḥammad ibn Mūsā al-Khwārizmī, **an algorithm is a set of repeatable processes that specify how to solve a type of problem.**

We use algorithms every day - and not just in marketing:

- Our morning routine is an algorithm, a set of repeatable processes we design to solve the problem of starting our days.

- I'd be willing to bet that you put the same general article of clothing on every morning.
- You brush your teeth in the same direction, starting on the same side of your mouth, every time.
- You consume your morning beverage of choice the same way, with the same set preferences and ingredients.
- All cooking recipes are essentially algorithms.

We use algorithms in every part of our lives, to solve the same types and classes of problems - regular, repeatable tasks that need predictable outcomes.

We think in algorithms. When we're faced with a challenge at work, the first thing we do is wrack our brains to determine whether we've solved this problem before - and if so, what the solution was. We've thought in algorithms since we were infants, children. Every child begins their life journey with a series of simple cause and effect algorithms - if this, then that. If I touch a hot stove, then it hurts. If I eat this vegetable, then Mom rewards me. Over time, our algorithms become more complex. Think about driving a car. Our algorithms start small and primitive - gas pedal, brake pedal, steering wheel. Over time, we learn, we evolve, and suddenly we're cruising down the highway with a doughnut in one hand, coffee in the other, yelling at our smartphone's hands-free features, and steering with our knees.

In marketing, we've been relying on - and fighting - algorithms since the dawn of digital marketing. Some of our earliest experiences with algorithms started in email marketing. In the late 1990s, email spam had become a rampant problem, so email vendors began creating spam detection algorithms. As marketers, we had to learn to adapt to these spam detection and spam blocking algorithms, from silly primitive tricks like changing the word "free" to something like "F*R*E*E" in subject lines to building sophisticated email deliverability models that help us predict list quality.

We've evolved our own algorithms as marketers. Any marketer who's done an A/B test with different subject lines in email marketing has used algorithms for the testing as well as algorithms to evaluate which test won.

* * *

Another area we faced as marketers confronting algorithms was in SEO, as we tried to figure out what pages ranked well in search engines. We developed our own algorithms for creating content to be found by search engines. Those with some grey hair remember the heady days of the late 1990s and early 2000s, putting every possible variation of keywords on our pages in white text on a white background in a 3-point font at the bottom of the page.

More recently, marketers have faced (and largely been defeated by) algorithms in social media. We reference these algorithms all the time - the Facebook News Feed algorithm, the Instagram algorithm, the Twitter algorithm, the YouTube Recommended Content algorithm. These algorithms try to keep users within social media platforms and punish marketers who make boring content. Any marketer who's been working with social media since 2012 remembers the days when more than 1% of our audiences actually saw our content without having to pay just to be seen.

Today, algorithms power virtually every

aspect of our digital experience, as both marketers and consumers. From directions on our smartphone's GPS mapping app to recommended purchases like "other customers who bought X also bought Y", algorithms dictate the reality we experience.

All algorithms used in machine learning and artificial intelligence are fundamentally rooted in statistics and mathematics, from the simplest predictive algorithms like linear regression - such as determining if one variable changes proportionally with another variable - to the most complex, sophisticated neural networks. If an algorithm is a recipe, statistical and mathematical techniques are the cooking techniques that form the basis of the recipe. Just as a recipe for a pot roast involves both braising and roasting, an algorithm can use multiple techniques to achieve its outcome.

The media tends to use the terms algorithm and model interchangeably, and they're not interchangeable terms. What's the difference?

As we just talked about, **an algorithm is a repeatable process**. It doesn't necessarily learn, nor does it need to be trained.

Algorithms are just repeatable processes; every piece of software uses them, so just because software has algorithms doesn't mean it's using machine learning or artificial intelligence.

An algorithm that does learn is more properly called a model. **Models are essentially pieces of software**, in the same way that Microsoft Word is a piece of software. When we talk about Facebook's News Feed algorithm, we're actually referring to the News Feed machine learning model.

The easiest way to differentiate the two is by a simple equation:

Algorithms + Data = Machine Learning Model

You'll hear in machine learning conversations a lot of references to "pre-trained models" and "fine-tuning models"; marketing AI vendors will often tell you that they have some kind of proprietary model they've built that they fine-tune when you become a customer. All they're saying is that they've got software which can learn from your data as well.

* * *

We'll dig into the different kinds of models in the next chapter, but for now, it's enough to know that models are algorithms combined with data. You can have algorithms without models, but you cannot have models without algorithms.

This brings us to one of the most important parts of machine learning for marketers: understanding the basic capabilities of what machine learning can do for you.

Types of Machine Learning

To understand machine learning's applications, we need to know a bit more about how machine learning works - what the major types of machine learning are, and how they apply to our marketing efforts. To better understand machine learning types, we must start with the kinds of data that machine learning models can learn from.

The two fundamental types of data we deal with all the time in machine learning are **numeric** and **non-numeric** data. This is relatively self-explanatory - numbers are numbers, and everything else that are not numbers, such as categories, dimensions, media, text, etc. In marketing applications like Google Analytics, you'll often hear these referred to as metrics and dimensions, but fundamentally, either our data is numeric or it isn't.

In machine learning, you'll hear these two types of data referred to as *continuous* (numeric) or *categorical* (non-numeric). Many types of data have blends of both; for example, a survey we run to our audiences will have continuous results (on a scale of 1 to 5, how much do you ...), as well as categorical results (open-ended questions like 'how was your last purchase?').

As marketers, we want to crunch both kinds of data, especially at scale. We need to process vast quantities of numbers every day (the Facebook Page export spreadsheet alone has a whopping 14 tabs of data). We also need to process the non-numeric data, such as emails, call center conversations, social media posts, etc.

Very often, we'll also need to transform our data from one kind to the other. For example, the day of the week is a non-numeric piece of information. To make this more useful, we might transform it into a count - instead of knowing a purchase was made on a Wednesday, we might tabulate how many purchases occurred on Wednesdays, or how many Wednesdays it took for a customer to convert. In the most sophisticated forms of machine learning, all the inputs must be numerical, so we see this transformation of non-numeric data into numeric data quite frequently.

* * *

So one way of categorizing the applications of machine learning is based on the kind of data we're working with. The second way to categorize the applications of machine learning is by the outcomes they generate.

Supervised Learning

Sometimes, we're looking for a known outcome. If, for example, we're using machine learning to find photos on Instagram of our logo, we have a clear outcome, a known result. We know what our logo looks like, so our machine learning efforts will focus on training the machine to recognize our logo in all sorts of conditions. This is a branch of machine learning called **supervised learning**.

What are some common marketing tasks that are ideally suited for supervised machine learning?

- Logo identification
- Mentions of us in social media
- Sentiment analysis
- Influencer identification
- Attribution analysis
- Parts of speech tagging

- Speech recognition
- Forecasting and prediction
- What makes content rank well for SEO
- Content summarization

All these tasks have known outcomes, so supervised machine learning can help us understand these outcomes in our data with greater speed and accuracy.

Unsupervised Learning

Sometimes, we don't know what outcome we're looking for. Instead, we need to know what sort of data we have. Imagine a box full of data - we'd want to understand what's in the box. For example, at the start of this book we referenced that there are, on average, more than a quarter million news stories every day. What are those stories about? What topics, people, events, etc. makes up those quarter million stories? We don't know what we're looking for, but we do know we want to organize the data so we can better understand and analyze it. Our machine learning efforts will focus on that kind of organization; this branch of machine learning is called **unsupervised learning**.

* * *

What are some common marketing tasks that are ideally suited for unsupervised machine learning?

- Sorting images and videos
- Understanding social media conversations about us, competitors, or our industry
- Analyzing company coverage to determine brand strength
- Clustering and sorting customers to find our best customers
- Digesting the day's headlines to find trending topics to write about

For example, a few years ago when I worked at a PR agency, I was heading to a client meeting with a request from the client to break down the coverage they'd received for a major client announcement. The team working on that account hadn't been able to read through more than a few of the thousands of articles written about the client, and the client wanted the big picture perspective, not just a handful of anecdotes.

Using an unsupervised learning technique called topic modeling, I fed the 2,621 articles about the client into the machine and had it distill down the major themes into 20 topics:

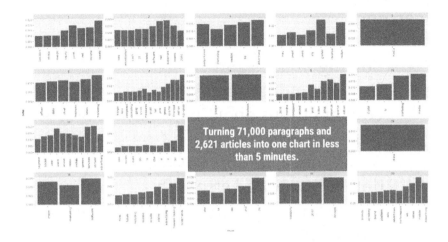

Turning 71,000 paragraphs and 2,621 articles into one chart in less than 5 minutes.

Instead of having to read all 2,621 articles, we could look at a single chart and understand with accuracy what the coverage was about. This alleviated the client's concerns that the PR team was hand-picking only favorable coverage as well; using machine learning, we delivered faster results that were also better results.

Each branch of machine learning has dozens, if not hundreds, of well-known techniques to help us achieve our aims of understanding and working with our data better. In the same way that major types of cooking, such as baking, frying, or broiling, contain many techniques, so does machine learning.

The Four Fundamental Problems and Solutions

When we gather our outcomes and data types, we find four fundamental problems that machine learning helps us solve:

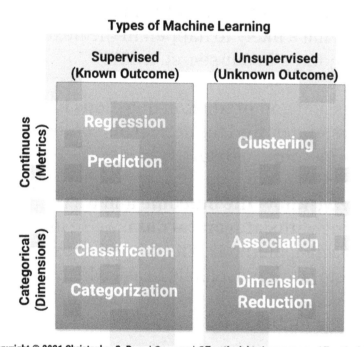

Types of Machine Learning

	Supervised **(Known Outcome)**	**Unsupervised** **(Unknown Outcome)**
Continuous **(Metrics)**	Regression Prediction	Clustering
Categorical **(Dimensions)**	Classification Categorization	Association Dimension Reduction

When we **know the outcome** and we're working with **continuous data**, we're using *regression and prediction* methods. The key questions marketers are most likely to ask which would be solved by regression and prediction include:

- What contributing variables led to this outcome, such as increased or decreased ROI?
- What was the sentiment of our social media coverage in the last year?
- Who is most influential in our industry?
- What's likely to happen in the next 12 months in our search traffic?

Regression and prediction questions help us understand or find numerical outcomes based on our numerical data.

When we **know the outcome** and we're working with **categorical data**, we're using *classification* methods. The key questions marketers are most likely to ask which would be solved by classification and categorization methods include:

- What topics are most prominent in news coverage about us?
- What have customers mentioned in their calls to our call center?
- What are our top influencers talking about overall?

- What are the subjects of the top million photos on Instagram?
- What are the major job titles of our customers in our CRM?

Classification and categorization questions help us to organize data we already have.

When we **don't know the outcome** and we're working with **continuous data**, we're using *clustering* methods. The key questions marketers are most likely to ask which would be solved by clustering include:

- What do our most profitable customers have in common?
- When customers buy a certain product, what else are they likely to buy?
- How frequently do negative complaints co-occur?
- What combinations of metrics lead to our best conversions?

Clustering helps us make order out of disorderly numeric data, showing patterns where we might not otherwise be able to see them.

Finally, when we **don't know the outcome** and

we're working with **categorical data**, we're going to tackle our problems with *association and dimension reduction*. The key questions marketers are most likely to ask which would be solved with dimension reduction methods include:

- Out of all these conversations, which ones should we pay attention to most?
- What do our customers really think of our brand?
- With all these data points, which ones really impact conversion and which are noise?

Dimension reduction helps us simplify very large amounts of data with no clear outcome, so that we're better able to start analyzing it.

Integrating Machine Learning Methods

Just as creating a great dinner requires more than one method of cooking, so too will we rarely use just one type of machine learning. Many of the problems we want to solve in marketing require combinations of types and techniques in order to find the answers we seek.

* * *

Often, we'll also alternate between categorical and continuous data, in order to understand the complexities of a problem.

Let's look at an example. Suppose we want to understand the perception of our brand better, using news coverage. How might we approach this problem? We'd first gather our data and see what was available. Let's use the coffee chain Starbucks as an example case, and use the Talkwalker media monitoring platform to extract the data.

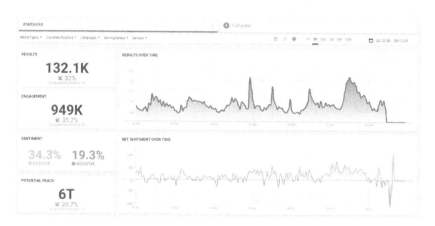

In just a week's news about the ubiquitous coffee shop, we've discovered 132,000 stories. We're not going to read all that; if an average news article's length is roughly 300 words, that's 39.6 million words to read - just in the last week. It would take us 110 days of reading at 250 words per minute to consume just a week's stories about Starbucks.

First, once we've gathered and prepared our data, we'll likely want to spend time understanding what's in it. We'd use *dimension reduction* to assess what data points to keep or discard. Should we look at all the stories, or just the stories that got a lot of reach? Is there a relationship between brand perception (the outcome we care about) and all the data about these different stories? Does story length matter? What about the individual publications? We'd want to reduce the hundreds or even thousands of different dimensions and metrics about news stories down to the ones that have statistical relevance to our goal.

We'd next use *categorization and classification* to organize and sort our data. What are the different formats? What about the different topics, different authors? Classifying the data into different categories will help us make sense of it and further weed out irrelevant stuff.

We'd then quantify our findings and use

clustering to find groups and communities of results, then regression to identify which clusters were most relevant. Stories about Starbucks moving into a plaza aren't necessarily relevant to the brand's perception. Stories about service, about coffee, about baristas - those are more likely to be relevant.

Once we found the most relevant, we'd go back to *categorization* to tease out more granular insights, then either cluster or use *regression* to bring greater specificity to that subset of insights. For example, if we narrow down the massive number of stories to just stories about baristas' service, we might then use machine learning to identify sentiment. Are people happy with the service they receive? If so, what language do they use to describe the service?

We'll dig more into these techniques in the chapter on practical applications so you can see examples written out, but this gives you a sense of the different ways we'd combine machine learning techniques together to achieve the outcome we're

Deep Learning

* * *

The process described above, combining supervised and unsupervised machine learning methods together, is awfully manual. What if there was a way to do some machine learning with our machine learning? That's what the third branch of machine learning is: deep learning. Deep learning is nothing more than the above process, but automated so that we don't have to individually choose the techniques necessary to distill down our data into usable outcomes.

Deep learning typically requires our data to be transformed entirely into numeric data (though most deep learning software does this automatically), then begins to process it towards a defined outcome, combining supervised and unsupervised techniques together. We don't get to offer much in the way of guidance when the machines build these models, and they can be very, very expensive in terms of computational costs, but when they work, they tend to work very well and scale very well to enormous data sets.

Deep learning shows up often in complex visual recognition tasks such as self-driving cars, as well as complex language tasks like translating one language to another. Because of the nature of how deep learning models work, they tend to do poorly with smaller datasets, just as a huge industrial blender wouldn't effectively be able to blend a tablespoon of butter. They need massive amounts of data to do their jobs well.

Before we continue, let's pause to have a word about data, the raw ingredient that powers all of machine learning and AI.

The Vital Importance of Good Data

In the last chapter, we looked at the basics of machine learning. Before we go any further, we need to have a pointed conversation about data.

Data is the fundamental raw material for machine learning. Remember that a machine learning model is algorithms + data. The old expression from classical computer science - garbage in, garbage out - is just as applicable to machine learning as it is to any other kind of programming.

If we continue our food analogies, no matter how skilled the chef or how fancy the appliances and tools, if the ingredients are bad, the food will be bad. No one can turn a loaf of moldy bread into a five-star sandwich. No one can uncurdle spoiled milk.

Similarly, any machine learning software which is fed bad data is going to create bad outcomes - if it creates anything at all. In order to reach the outcomes we seek, we need our data to be good.

* * *

And as we said at the start of the book, marketing's data tends to be... less than stellar in quality. From junk spammed into our contact forms to people doing the bare minimum possible to keep our CRM software up to date to vendors constantly changing how data is collected, it's a wonder we accomplish anything with our data - and the reason why so few CMOs use data to make decisions. It's not that they don't believe in the power of data-driven marketing - it's that they know their data is filled with junk.

What's worse is that bad data, when used in machine learning, also tends to corrupt good data. Imagine taking all your ingredients and putting them in a blender (which is how some deep learning models work). If even a fraction of the ingredients are rotten, how will that whole batch taste? You'll know something is wrong with even a tiny amount of rotten product.

For example, suppose we are trying to predict which email domains are likely to unsubscribe from our email lists, and we've got a bunch of mis-typed emails like gmial.com and hotmial.com. Even something as simple as counting how many of each domain there is will be thrown off by this obviously crap data. Creating a model that tries to predict based off these domains could inadvertently start guessing that gmail.com and hotmail.com are also bad, potentially ruining our email marketing lists.

So, good data is imperative if we want our machine learning and AI efforts to succeed. What constitutes good data? At Trust Insights, we measure data quality by six factors, the 6C Data Quality Framework.

The 6C Data Quality Framework

Clean
· Prepared well, free of errors

Calculable
· Must be workable and usable by business users

Complete
· No missing information

Quality Data

Credible
· Must be collected in a valid way

Comprehensive
· Must cover the questions being asked

Chosen
· No irrelevant/confusing data

* * *

Good data should be:

- Clean
- Complete
- Comprehensive
- Chosen
- Credible
- Calculable

Let's explore each of these facets of good data.

Clean. Clean data is data that is prepared and free of errors, free of "dirt". Dirty data would be data with anomalies, or contaminated. This includes correctness - data that's incorrect is not clean. A common marketing example of unclean data is that person putting test@test.com in your website forms. That data is dirty because it's intentionally wrong. Unintentionally wrong data litters our marketing software as well - how many people have johnsmith@hotmial.com or other misspelled data in their systems?

Complete. Complete data has no critical missing information. Some machine learning algorithms do very poorly or outright break if data is missing, so a major part of preparing data for machine learning includes ensuring its completeness. If data is missing, either it's non-critical or it can be imputed (inferred) correctly. A common example of incomplete data is website analytics data during site moves; companies often forget to copy their tracking codes like Google Analytics to their new site for a day or two, and data goes missing. Even something as simple as doing a month over month or year over year comparison will be thrown off by a single day of missing data.

Comprehensive. One of the biggest challenges of many datasets is that they answer a narrow question but may not answer bigger picture questions that are logical next steps, so data must be comprehensive. For example, suppose we're looking at data about social media analytics. A logical question is, so what business impact did social media have? That requires data typically not stored in social media analytics, which means a comprehensive dataset should also include data from down the funnel.

Chosen. Just as completeness mandates we have enough data, chosen data mandates that we not have too much data. More data isn't necessarily better; we need to choose our data appropriately so that we're answering the questions we need to answer without adding noise. Some machine learning algorithms get exponentially more expensive (in terms of processing time) as dataset grow larger, so we want to choose our data well. For example, in influencer marketing, there will always be tons of people who just talk to the ether, posting and sharing and tweeting even if no one's listening to them. We'd want to weed these pointless noisemakers out - leaving them in our dataset could pollute it if we're trying to understand the topics that tastemakers are talking about.

Credible. The process of collecting the data is just as important as the data itself. How credible is the data? What's its lineage, its provenance? Was it collected in a manner that is free of bias? This is especially important any time we're collecting data from human beings (as opposed to other computer systems). If we don't actively screen our data for bias, we risk feeding our human flaws to our machines. An example of this happened in 2018: Amazon had to scrap an AI-powered HR system because the data it trained on was heavily biased to hire male developers, and inherited that bias for its predictions about which job candidates to hire.

Calculable. Finally, data must be in a calculable, usable format that's accessible to machines and business users alike. Data stored in an obscure or difficult format is less likely to be used than data that is readily accessible or transformable for non-data scientists. Certainly, we should store and manage it in whatever format is most cost-effective and efficient, but with an eye towards ease of use. Many enterprise systems store data in such complex structures that it's nearly impossible for a line of business manager to extract a quick answer in order to make a decision - and that reduces the value of the data significantly. A number of years ago, we worked with a major technology company whose sales department prohibited - PROHIBITED - marketing from receiving or analyzing sales data, likely because they were terrible at sales. What did this do to marketing's attempts to build scoring models and predictive forecasts about what marketing was working? Obviously it completely ruined any such efforts.

Use these 6 criteria as is, like a scorecard, to manage your data, especially as you embark on any kind of statistics, data science, or machine learning project. Every data source should have scores associated with it, as well as any notes or annotations from the data sources. Some tools, like Google Analytics, allow users to store notes right inside the data, like "updated the website today, forgot the tracking code for 6 hours" so that future data analysis can be adjusted appropriately. Consider even putting the scorecard in the documentation of your data, like a nutrition label.

So, we've tackled the concepts of machine learning, how it works at a high level, key questions, and prerequisites. Let's start diving into practical applications of machine learning and AI for marketers.

Now that we have a basic understanding of the broad categories of techniques in AI and machine learning, let's begin examining some more specific techniques and use cases in depth.

Let's look at five key marketing problems that most of us face, and the machine learning techniques used to solve those problems.

Problem 1: Marketing is unfocused. We don't know what's working and what's not - we have no shortage of data. What we have is a shortage of actionable insights, of what to focus on.

Problem 2: Marketing is unclear. We don't know what to prioritize, especially in data-rich disciplines like SEO.

Problem 3: Marketing data is untapped. All that data is like panning for gold. We don't know what's in our data, so we can't make the most of it. It's like being handed an entire grocery store all at once.

* * *

Problem 4: Marketing is unprepared. We spend most of our time in reactive mode, reacting to and trying to deal with the fires in our inboxes instead of being proactive, planning ahead and forecasting what's likely to happen so we're not caught unaware.

Problem 5: Marketing to the unknown. When it comes to people - customers, audiences, influencers - we don't know who's who. We may invest our time and effort in all the wrong places, in all the wrong people.

For each of these problems, we could use machine learning to speed up our time and efforts towards reaching solutions.

It almost goes without saying that the universe of machine learning techniques is far greater than a mere five, but these five problems and solutions are use cases that you're very likely to run into.

Problem 1: Marketing is unfocused

It's surely obvious that we're swimming - no, drowning - in marketing data, and we need to make better decisions, faster. **The generally accepted best practice for focusing our marketing is attribution analysis** - understanding what strategies, tactics, and tools deliver the best results for our marketing.

There are many ways to do attribution analysis, but most of them, to be perfectly frank, kind of suck. We're all familiar with basics like last-touch attribution (where the last thing the customer did gets all the credit) or first-touch attribution, but we seldom look past those two models for deeper answers.

The challenge with these models is something we know intuitively as customers. We don't buy like that for anything more than simple transactional interactions. Sure, we may make spur of the moment purchases for low risk items like a pack of chewing gum or a special item on an end cap at the grocery store, but for the most part, our purchasing patterns are more complex. We ask friends. We read reviews. We Google for more information. We receive emails.

In short, we do lots of things even for relatively simple purchases.

Here's a simple sanity check: how many emails in your inbox are from companies that you made relatively simple transactional purchases from? That shows you the power of many touches to spur consumer behavior - but we don't measure our marketing that way.

Why don't we? Because of the complexity of trying to do an analysis like that. Imagine taking every single interaction, from every single customer, and trying to build a model of what things caused a customer to convert, and in what order. You could do that if you had a handful of customers but once you reach dozens, or hundreds, or thousands, you simply can't. Doing a single analysis of your data with that many customers would take you so many years that by the time you were done, you might have hit retirement age.

Machine learning helps with attribution modeling by taking into account all these interactions from hundreds or thousands of customers and assigning them partial credit. The analogy I often use when explaining this is that of a baseball game. Who is the most valuable player on a baseball team? The pitcher? The slugger? The outfielder? The reality is that in baseball, every player has to make a substantial contribution for the team to win. You can't win a baseball game with a strong pitcher and a weak batting lineup; at best, you'll tie because you strike out the opposing team but your own team can't score. You can't win a baseball game with a power hitting roster and a team that can't catch anything. You need great players all around.

The same is true of our marketing. ***Despite years of batting around phrases like "omni-channel", we still don't view our marketing holistically***. We still see every channel as its own silo, its own little universe, when we should see every channel as a player on the team, trying to win the game together.

How does machine learning help us? We can't realistically put together every possible interaction that someone has with our properties, even in an era when we've got all the data and it's easier than ever. The global pandemic of 2020-2021 forced everything to digital, so even offline things went online and permanently changed consumer behaviors. That means more data than ever. Machine learning techniques help us sequence the data and understand what channels help us convert.

Here's an example. Suppose we have three customer interactions that look like the following:

A: Email > Facebook > Search > No purchase
B: Email > Twitter > Facebook > Search > Purchase
C: Email > Search > Purchase
D: Email > Twitter > Purchase

What should get credit? Using machine learning techniques, our machines could look at each of these examples and give weights to every interaction. This is a drastic oversimplification, but it gets the idea across. A negative interaction - meaning a conversion didn't happen - would earn a -1 score. So here's the same analysis, with numbers:

* * *

A: -1 > -1 > -1
B : 1 > 1 > 1 > 1 > 1
C: 1 > 1
D: 1 > 1

Now, if we tally up everything, we'd get the following:

Email: 2
Facebook: 0
Search: 1
Twitter: 2

In this oversimplified example, email and Twitter would have the largest net positive scores, followed by search, then Facebook. The actual machine learning technique that would deliver these results, Markov chain modeling, also takes into account the probability of one step leading to another as part of its model, such that Email > Twitter are not the same as Twitter > Email, which is not reflected in the example above.

When we apply this particular technique to our marketing data, we begin to understand which channels are most likely to lead to conversions we care about. Here's an example from my personal website:

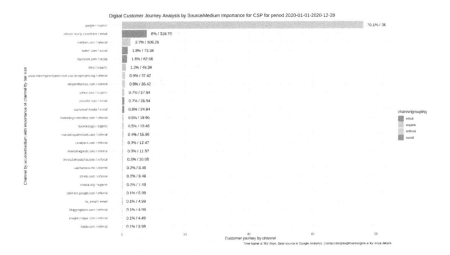

From this example, I can clearly see that organic search drives the vast majority of conversions on my website, followed by my newsletter, medium.com, then Twitter and Facebook. What's more, because Markov chain modeling accounts for sequences, I can plot this out on a timeline as to what's closer to the beginning of the buyer's journey or the end of the journey:

* * *

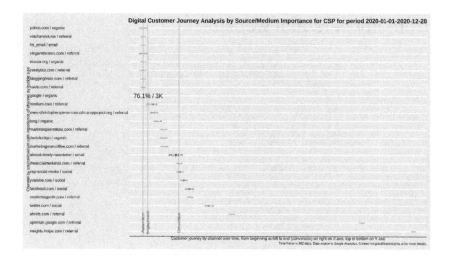

This tells me that organic search is an awareness driver for my site, while email and social media are closers. From this information, I understand better the role of each channel - and I know where I need to add focus if I want to change my marketing for the better.

For example, suppose my marketing funnel is full at the top of the funnel (it is) and relatively empty near the bottom (it is). Using these two analysis, I know that I need to spend some time on Twitter and Facebook nudging people to take action. Those channels aren't awareness builders - people who interact with me there know who I am already, so I shouldn't waste time trying to re-introduce myself. Instead, I should be nudging them to do something that provides business value.

This is how we use machine learning to focus our marketing, to help us understand what's working and what isn't working. We can take the same technique and apply it in multiple different scenarios. For example, suppose I want to look at how the different pages on my website interact. Do some pages naturally nudge people towards conversion more than others?

A number of years ago, there was an apocryphal tale of a university that didn't install sidewalks on its new campus. For a year, they let students just wander the campus, and then after that year, they paved over all the places where paths were naturally worn into the grass, creating a campus that felt natural and comfortable.

The same concept applies to our websites. There are some pages people naturally visit in a certain order before converting, and other pages that don't perform nearly as well. Using the same Markov chain modeling technique, we can plot out which pages those are:

* * *

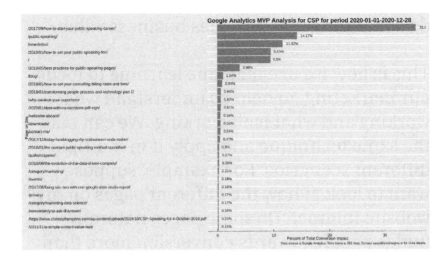

Now, instead of wondering which pages to optimize on our website, we have a punchlist of the most important, most valuable pages. These are the pages we should be A/B testing on. These are the pages we should re-optimize often. These are the pages we should be promoting on social media, in email newsletters, and in our advertising.

Machine learning brings our marketing into focus.

Google Analytics is one of my favorite pieces of software. Yet as robust as it is, I don't look at most of the data in it. If you sit down and count, in version 3 of the software, there are 510 different metrics and dimensions (numbers and non-numeric data points) available to us.

Here's the challenging question: **which of the 510 numbers matter most?**

Explore the depths of any system you use in marketing - your marketing automation software, your CRM, even your social media accounts. There's so much data, so many data points - which ones should we pay attention to?

Here's a painful example. Anyone who has ever run a Facebook Page is familiar with Facebook's Page Insights. One of the options we have as Page managers is the ability to export our data for offline analysis. For just one single Facebook Page, we end up with a spreadsheet with 24 tabs, each with up to 232 columns of data. If books supported animated GIFs, there'd be one of John Cleese frowning disapprovingly right here.

Out of those 24 tabs and up to 232 columns, which ones actually matter?

We could guess, of course. Some are intuitive - clicks on links we share probably matter because we're measuring how much traffic we send from Facebook to something we own, like our website. But what about everything else?

We have two machine learning techniques at our disposal to help winnow this gigantic mess down to something manageable. The first technique is called dimension reduction, and it uses the power of statistics to help us remove stuff that simply doesn't matter. Most modern data science software tools allow us to apply very common cleaning functions to a dataset and remove obvious junk, part of the data preparation process.

The second technique is called feature selection, which is part of running advanced regression analysis. Let's take a quick tour of what this process might look like, and how an experienced, technical marketer might accomplish it. An important note, before we start the tour, is that I wouldn't expect someone without a technical background to be able to do this, nor is it something you have to do on a frequent basis. It's one of those techniques you pull out before a quarterly board review or at your semi-annual planning sessions, not something you do every week.

Why are we walking through a tour, if I don't expect you to do it? So that you understand how the process works and can direct or manage someone to be able to do it for you.

Walkthrough Example

Let's take our Facebook data as a starting point. I've got the comma-separated values (CSV) file from my Facebook Page that tells me how my Page performed. It's 157 rows and 48 columns wide - pretty hefty for a single channel. Our first step would be to remove stuff like empty rows and columns, a fairly common occurrence with social media data. That knocks out 3 columns of junk that Facebook gave us.

Next, there are some metrics which are just zeroes all the way down. Not very helpful, so those should go away. That erases an additional 19 metrics. If I were running a lot of paid ads of different types, those 19 metrics might have stuff in them, but for the purpose of this exercise, we're discarding them because they're empty and offer no analytical value.

As a side note, this is why the process can't fully be automated. Every company is different and uses its tools differently, so some knowledge of both the data and the company behind the data are essential to deal with the nearly infinite variations that occur.

A next step is to identify functional duplicates, or high correlates. For the kind of analysis we're trying to do, having duplicates is bad - it's just confusing. A functional duplicate is when two variables march in lockstep - usually because one variable is contained in another. Again, this is something that offers no real analytical value. If page views and sessions march in lockstep, you probably don't need one of them.

If we examine a chart of correlations for my Facebook Page, we see that some variables are insanely highly correlated - 0.95 or higher:

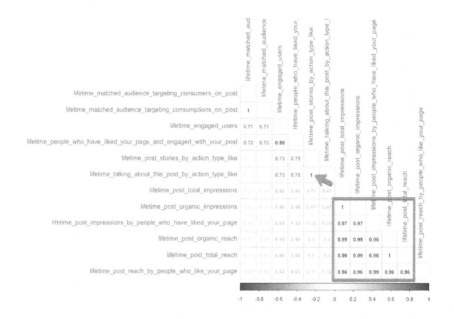

When you see these kinds of crazy high correlations, it means you've got serious overlap, and is it any surprise when you look at the variables? Lifetime post organic reach and lifetime post total reach are redundant. Lifetime post total reach includes lifetime post organic reach. They should march in lockstep for my account (but they wouldn't for an account that relied heavily on boosted posts and sponsored content). So when we run into situations like this, part of the puzzle is deciding what to keep and what to get rid of.

* * *

Since I do almost no advertising (which would push up the total impressions numbers), it's safe to say that organic and total anything should be almost perfectly correlated. I'll remove the total versions of the variables in this case. If you ran a Facebook page that had substantial advertising, you might choose differently.

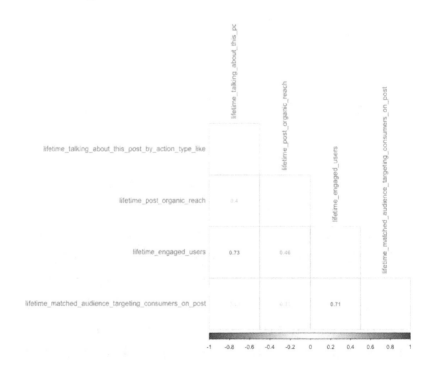

That leaves us with a much smaller number of variables to work with - four. That brings us to the next step in our process, the use of a regression technique to confirm which of the variables matters most to the outcome we care about. In this case, based on the data Facebook has shared in this dataset, I'm going to pick **lifetime post organic reach**. Based on the chart above, we already see that **lifetime engaged users** has the highest basic correlation to the outcome we care about, but for purposes of illustration, we'll use a more thorough procedure.

Using a machine learning algorithm called extreme gradient boosting, or XGBoost, we'll feed our refined Facebook dataset into the algorithm to create a model. Recall that **a machine learning model is data + algorithms**, so the final outcome of this will be both useful insights and a piece of software we could use on an ongoing basis if we needed to.

* * *

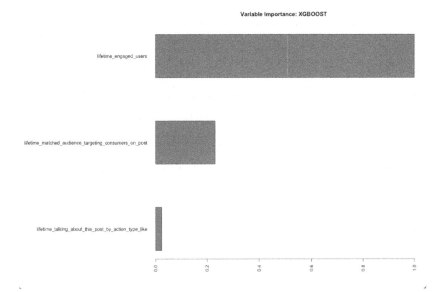

Sure enough, the XGBoost algorithm created a model which shows that **lifetime engaged users** is the key to getting more **lifetime post organic reach**.

What do you do with this information? In my case, I would focus more on getting engaged users. I'd tag people in Facebook posts from my page. I'd put up memes to encourage reactions. I'd ask questions, run polls and quizzes, anything it took to generate more engaged users, in order to achieve my outcome of increased organic reach for my posts.

Again, this is very much overkill, but this

recipe is how you boil down insanely large, complex datasets into things that matter. Now imagine doing this same exercise but with all the variables in your Google Analytics, tested against what delivers more conversions. Wouldn't it be great to know which channels really matter, or which pages on your website, or whether things like bounce rate or time on page matter or not?

The value above and beyond the analysis itself is knowing what works for your company. You'll read on a lot of content marketing blogs about experts' opinions on bounce rates in general, but your company might be different. Bounce rate might not matter to conversions on your site - or it might matter a great deal. Only by running analyses like the one above can you make that determination about whether any given metric should matter to you or not.

Problem 3: Marketing data is untapped

We've got no shortage of data. None whatsoever, and chances are, we even probably have a fair amount of really good data. The question is, are we using it effectively? Are we tapping into it for valuable insights?

The answer is almost certainly no, we're not. Consider some of the following data sources, and ask how well you're extracting usable insights from them:

- Customer phone calls
- Online reviews
- Social media conversations
- Customer service chats
- Your customer service inbox
- Conference and event conversations
- Sales phone calls
- Sales conversations
- Sales CRM notes

If you're extracting usable, actionable insights from any of these data sources on a regular, frequent basis, congratulations. You are in a rare minority of marketers. For the most part, marketers don't sufficiently use information from any of these sources. Why? Four reasons.

First, **the data itself is unstructured**. Text is by nature a highly variable, unstructured medium with incredible diversity, from simple one-emoji replies to massive, expletive-laden missives from customers. Turning unstructured data into structured data and then quantitative, numeric data is extremely difficult for most marketers.

Second, **the data is gigantic**. How many emails are in your customer service inbox? Hundreds? Thousands? Millions? Depending on the size of your organization, the latter is a real possibility.

Third, **the data is locked away** in many different formats. Customer service calls are probably audio recordings. Your chatbots probably store their data in a database of some kind. Your CRM has its own proprietary format that may be easy or difficult to work with. Your sales conversations are probably recorded Zoom calls or chicken scratch on the back of a bar napkin, snapped with a smartphone by the dim glow of a Pabst Blue Ribbon bar sign.

* * *

Fourth, the **technology to unlock the data** in each of these different formats may not be readily accessible to everyone - yet.

Thankfully, machine learning is helping us chip away at these four problems, particularly with a family of technologies called natural language processing. Natural language processing takes text data and helps us understand and quantify it. Combined with other technologies such as voice recognition, we can boil down incredibly large amounts of heterogenous data into numeric analyses we make decisions from.

Walkthrough Example

Let's walk through an example or two to see how these technologies play out. In our first scenario, let's say we're monitoring a known hashtag in our community or industry on Twitter. Despite having lost some of its luster since the early days, Twitter is still a useful, valuable data source for many industries. For our example, we'll look at the #MarketingTwitter hashtag, a popular community hashtag.

* * *

In just a month of data, we've got over 10,602 unique, distinct posts to weed through. How do we turn this pile of data into usable information? As with the previous example, I don't expect you to pick up R or Python and immediately start writing code to process data; this is a walkthrough to understand the process, the thinking involved, and how you might be able to manage or direct either an employee or a vendor to assist you with it.

The first step we take with any dataset is to understand it. What's in the box?

```
marketing_tweets_df        10602 obs. of 12 variables
  created_at : POSIXct[1:10602], format: "2020-12-09 14:05:29" "2020-12-09 20:10:35" "2020-12-18 17:16:
  screen_name : chr [1:10602] "JoeGGarrison" "baublesnbraids" "gmz_stephanie" "Kammie_Jenkins" ...
  source : chr [1:10602] "Twitter Web App" "Twitter for iPhone" "Twitter for iPhone" "Twitter Web App"
  favorite_count : num [1:10602] 522 487 404 281 259 246 243 226 218 218 ...
  retweet_count : num [1:10602] 6 1 8 0 4 1 15 12 1 13 ...
  description : chr [1:10602] "Ministry guy turned marketer. Tweet marketing, music, dad jokes, with a
  url : chr [1:10602] "https://t.co/tggqf1QC7m" "https://t.co/xaWJ9mQQ3C" NA NA ...
  followers_count: num [1:10602] 1140 962 238 4733 1618 ...
  friends_count : num [1:10602] 928 1397 189 800 1273 ...
  listed_count : num [1:10602] 47 229 10 118 60 25 469 10 128 102 ...
  text : chr [1:10602] "Hey, #MarketingTwitter! Raise your hand \U0001f64b  if you DON'T have a market
  status_id : num [1:10602] 1.34e+18 1.34e+18 1.34e+18 1.34e+18 1.34e+18 ...
```

We've got 12 fields to work with - the date a tweet was posted, the screen name, the device used, how many favorites and retweets a post earned, the users's description, the tweet URL, the poster's followers, friends, and list counts, the status ID, and most critical for this exercise, what the text of the post was.

* * *

Let's look at the text and start with something very simple - a word count. What words show up most?

	feature	frequency
1	#marketingtwitter	10612
2	to	6382
3	the	5742
4	a	5277
5	and	4640
6	for	3491
7	of	3382
8	you	3334
9	i	3161
10	this	3154
11	in	2841
12	#marketing	2688
13	is	2340
14	on	2203
15	about	2140
16	marketing	2048

Well, that's not super illuminating. Part of the reason is we've got a ton of junk words, called stop words, which are basically filler - to, the, a, and, etc. Part of unlocking the value of text with natural language processing is the refining process that goes into cleaning up text - it's like panning for gold. You have to sift out a lot of dirt to find the gold. Let's repeat the analysis but removing common stop words.

	feature	frequency
1	#marketingtwitter	10612
2	#marketing	2688
3	marketing	2048
4	@charlesfrize	1313
5	#digitalmarketingservices	1279
6	#onlinemarketingtopeurope	1271
7	#onlinemarketingghana	1246
8	reading	1239
9	#frizemedia	1224
10	amp	870
11	social	789
12	#digitalmarketing	768
13	new	748
14	@thatchristinag	711
15	people	636

* * *

That's a little better. It's still not something that's valuable or even useful. One of the characteristics of language is that important words typically don't go it alone; they're often in combination with others. For example, Google and analytics are separate, independent words but take on a different meaning when put together - Google Analytics, the product. If we go back through our data and look for the most common combinations, we might see something different.

* * *

	feature	frequency
1	social_media	354
2	digital_marketing	129
3	reading_tips	79
4	im_looking	75
5	new_year	74
6	hi_im	70
7	can_help	58
8	dont_miss	55
9	digital_marketer	49
10	please_dm	49
11	youd_like	49
12	youre_looking	48
13	make_money	47
14	put_together	47
15	reply_tweet	46

This is definitely better, this look at the different commonly occurring phrases. We're starting to see some phrases that make logical sense - and also starting to see a bigger problem with this dataset. It's clogged with spammers hijacking the hashtag to promote their stuff.

* * *

Fortunately, spammers lack something that legitimate accounts tend to have in abundance: real conversations and interactions. Finding those conversational strings uses a technique called TF-IDF, which is short for text frequency/inverse document frequency, a mathematical technique designed to clean out repetitive junk from a body of text and identify those terms that tend to stand out.

Sure enough, once we focus on conversations as opposed to self-promotional jerks, we see the conversation change.

* * *

	name	value
1	social_media	514.14646
2	digital_marketing	248.81460
3	reading_tips	167.56480
4	im_looking	160.77294
5	can_help	130.80581
6	youre_looking	120.00895
7	digital_marketer	114.09672
8	marketing_training	106.44696
9	media_marketing	105.39985
10	social_media_marketing	105.39985
11	content_marketing	104.95021
12	id_love	98.64258
13	graphic_designer	97.10544
14	diverse_voices	96.66562
15	new_year	94.67780

In fact, a key insight we're beginning to see here is that an awful lot of real conversations on #MarketingTwitter are people looking for training around social media marketing and content marketing. That's a useful insight - doubly so if we were a company that offered training in those areas! By mining the conversations, we've unlocked some value. Let's dig a little deeper.

Using a technique called vectorization, we're able to dig deeper into the mathematical relationships between words. The challenge with what we've done so far is that our analyses have relied on words occurring together to determine relationships. For example, we understand intuitively that social media marketing and Facebook marketing or your Facebook page go together. But looking at the word lists above, we don't necessarily see that. Vectorization techniques would notice that every time we talk about social media, somewhere nearby, a Facebook-related word or phrase appears, and thus the two should be shown together because they're related.

With this technique, what can we tell about our Twitter conversations?

* * *

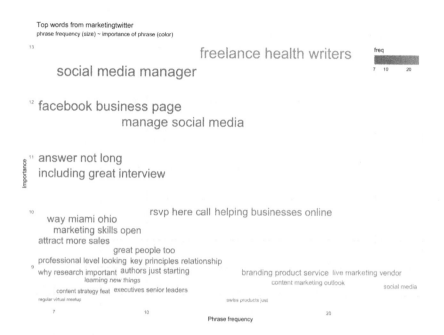

Top words from marketingtwitter
phrase frequency (size) ~ importance of phrase (color)

We see exactly that - the bigger, redder terms are more important in the conversation and more frequent when placed in a bigger context using vectorization. The conversations about social media marketing are almost exclusively about Facebook Business Pages - and that tells us where our conversation participants' heads are.

If we were a social media training company, we'd now have zeroed in on the pain point that people are talking about - training on how to manage a Facebook Business Page. From there, we could meaningfully participate in the conversation and offer real value without having to read through all 10,601 tweets.

Multimedia Walkthrough Example

Let's kick things up a notch with a second walkthrough. A little while ago, Conversion Interactive Agency hired us to help them diagnose what was going on with their Indeed.com job ads for recruiting truck divers. They weren't performing as well as they thought the ads should have been performing.

We started by ingesting all 5,000 of their ads from Indeed.com and performed the exact same kind of analysis on their ad copy as we did with the Twitter conversations above:

* * *

We see pretty clearly what their ads are about - "here's everything you need to have to qualify for our positions", the class of drivers license, specific truck types, etc.

The real question is, why weren't these ads performing? We were given access to 17,000 voice recordings from their call center, calls where a recruiter was talking with the candidates, doing interviewing. Using machine learning-powered voice transcription software, we turned all 17,000 calls into text transcripts, bringing them to a common format.

When we ran the conversation transcripts through the same vectorization analysis, we ended up with this analysis:

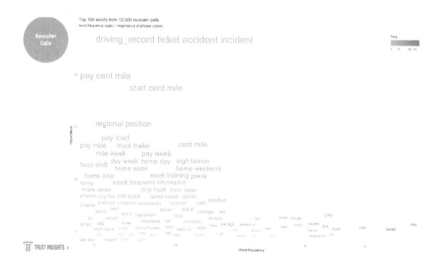

* * *

Well, well, well. What we see here are very different conversations. Drivers talked about pay per mile, whether they're home on the weekends, signing bonuses, how long their shifts are... all things that aren't mentioned in the job ads at all.

The problem became immediately clear: **candidates weren't responding to the job ads because the ads talked about nothing they cared about**. The ads served the company, but not the drivers. When the agency changed the ad copy to also include driver concerns, performance exploded, from 3,000 applications a month to 5,500 applications a month, a 67% increase in conversions in just 2 months with no change in budget.

Imagine getting 67% more ROI on anything in marketing. You'd be dancing in your chair. Your boss might be doing an equally awkward dance just outside your office space, which would be embarrassing but the bonus you both received would make up for it.

That's the power of tapping into the data you already have, especially unstructured data.

Chances are, the insights you need to make changes are already in your data. The challenge is unlocking those insights and then taking dramatic, rapid action on them.

Problem 4: Marketing is unprepared

Just about two months before the end of our fiscal year, whenever it is, we all go through the same inevitable exercise. We're asked to put together a strategic plan for the year ahead, along with a budget and our best guess for what resources we're going to need.

We typically dread those exercises, because they're usually a complete waste of time. We submit our best guesses and then either get beaten up when our forecasts don't match reality, or are told the powers that be have decided on an arbitrary number that also doesn't match reality.

Why does this exercise, and exercises similar to it, hurt so much? It's because we - humans - are typically very bad at prediction and forecasting. We overemphasize the short term and underemphasize the long term. We're not terribly good at taking data and extrapolating it forward in mathematically sound ways; at best, we give reasonable guesses. At worst, we just make stuff up and hope things break our way.

* * *

Forecasting has hit some rough times especially recently, what with a global pandemic that has disrupted everything. But even in the midst of great confusion, some things remain constant. The basics of life go on, even if the details get murky with all the chaos.

For example, major holidays still happen, and the behaviors that lead up to major holidays are still consistent. People still searched for gift guides leading up to the holidays in 2020 despite it being a completely atypical year in most respects:

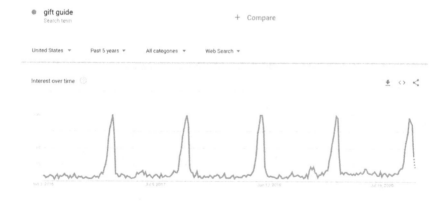

People may have searched a little less than previous years, but the behavior was still consistent enough that, had you been able to forecast ahead back in the summer, you would have known when to start publishing your holiday gift guide if you were a retailer.

So, if forecasting still works, how do we do it? The good news is that forecasting isn't some mysterious, dark, arcane art. We've been forecasting with varying degrees of accuracy since we could first communicate as a species. The difference today is that machines help us generate better forecasts from more complex data, forecasts that would take us so long to generate by hand that by the time we were done, the period we were forecasting would be over.

To forecast effectively, we need a few things.

First, **we need regular data**. Regular data is data that has some kind of seasonality or cyclicality to it. The above example of a holiday gift guide is a forecast that's easy to make because it's incredibly regular. The holidays happen at the same time every year, and the searches for gift guides tend to follow in lockstep.

Second, **we need data for things that have already happened**. We can't forecast things that have never happened before, which is why, even with the most powerful machine learning software, no one was able to predict the rise of COVID-19 or the outcome of the 2020 presidential election beforehand:

No one can forecast things that have never happened.

Third, **we need lots of very granular data** to forecast well. The less data there is, the less accurate and robust the forecast; if you have only quarterly data, you can only forecast in quarters, and you need many, many quarters of data in the past to forecast forward. The general rule of thumb with forecasting data is that for every 1 period forward you want to forecast, you need at least 4 periods of back data - and even then, you can run into issues. Five years of daily data is a robust dataset to forecast from. Five years of yearly data? That's only 5 data points, and you won't get much of a forecast.

The gold standard for forecasting over time is an algorithm called ARIMA, or auto-regressive integrated moving averages. From a computational perspective, it's actually a fairly primitive algorithm that barely qualifies as machine learning (though many companies such as Facebook have enhanced it with more sophisticated sub-analyses), and yet it still performs very well with some kinds of data.

Let's take a spin through how these forecasts might work and how you'd make use of them.

Walkthrough

We begin with some kind of regular, time-based data. In this case, I'm going to use the data from my email marketing system, the number of opens/read emails per email newsletter. What I'd like to know is what kind of readership I can forecast forward. This will help me better budget resources, as well as make decisions about sponsorships and advertisers.

* * *

As always, let's start by looking at the data. What do we see?

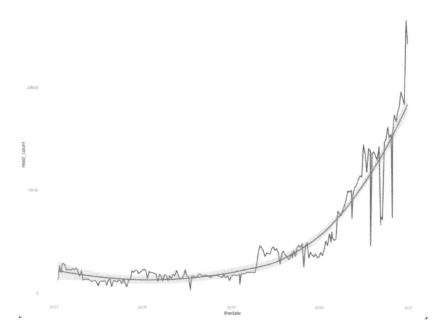

First, do we have clean data? It looks like it, yes. There are a couple of anomalies - those big dips in 2020 - but for the most part, we see very clean data. There aren't any major missing gaps or super weird spikes. I've added a red trend line so we can see what the general trend looks like as well. I've got about 4 full years of data here, so projecting forward for a year seems like something that should be reasonable.

* * *

We'll feed this into forecasting software and have it run 52 weeks ahead, to see what the year ahead looks like for my newsletter:

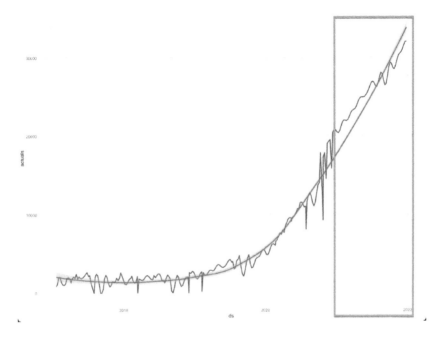

What we see, based on extrapolating from the past few years of data, is a clear linear increase of opens over the next year, with some rougher spots in the second half of the year and smooth sailing for the most part in the first half of the year. We sustain the momentum from 2020.

This forecast lets me know that growth is likely to continue, and thus if I'm selling ad space, I can offer to advertisers a certain amount of likely visibility and clicks as part of their ad package.

While taking existing marketing metrics and forecasting them forward is useful for budgeting and planning, we really kick things up a notch when we start to use it for content planning. Using the same algorithm, but substituting search data in place of email marketing data, we can take a look at when search volume for specific terms and keywords is likely to increase.

Let's take a basket of terms around different kinds of courses such as data science course, AI course, etc. and see what the future looks like:

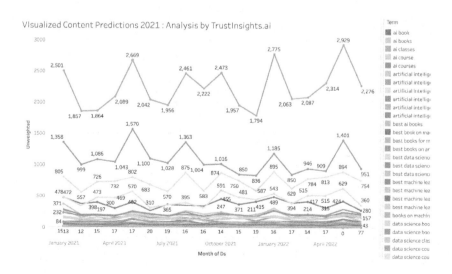

* * *

What this chart tells us are the periods of time in the coming year when individual search terms related to data science books and course are likely to spike in popularity. In turn, it's logical to conclude that's when audience interest will be highest in these topics - which means we'd better step up our marketing to be present and visible during those times. Let's dig a little deeper and see what this data looks like at a weekly level.

Content Predictions 2021

Term	January ..	January ..	January ..	January ..	January ..	February..	February..	February..	February..	March 7,..	March 1..
				Week of Ds							
data science course	464.6	536.2	550			417.3	441.4	487.4	510.6	491.9	455.2
machine learning course	244.1	289.5	308	January 17, 2021		213.9	234.1	268.6	282.3	270.6	259.2
data science courses	163.6	174.1	168.3	154.5	144.0	140.8	140.4	138.4	137.7	146.8	169.3
artificial intelligence course	128.1	104.3	80.5	76.7	88.7	96.0	87.6	75.9	80.1	102.4	124.3
machine learning books	90.0	90.0	90.6	96.3	104.8	106.5	97.0	85.2	85.3	98.7	110.4
ai courses	42.2	47.4	48.2	47.1	47.6	49.2	48.6	43.9	38.9	39.1	45.1
machine learning book	37.9	49.3	62.6	68.9	64.3	53.7	46.3	46.9	52.0	55.2	53.2
machine learning pdf	40.3	57.6	84.7	99.2	89.1	63.9	44.1	40.5	46.7	50.0	46.2
machine learning courses	57.9	63.3	59.3	48.3	38.6	35.7	37.4	39.3	40.3	43.1	48.4
best machine learning books	22.6	22.1	27.7	34.9	37.4	33.9	29.6	30.5	36.8	42.8	43.4
ai course	30.1	33.8	36.3	35.3	32.1	30.3	32.1	35.9	38.3	36.8	32.5
data science books	21.6	30.9	38.5	39.2	34.2	28.8	27.1	28.2	28.2	26.0	24.7
ai books	33.8	28.6	28.9	32.2	33.5	31.0	26.9	24.2	23.7	24.4	25.8
machine learning papers	16.2	16.5	15.7	16.0	19.6	24.6	26.9	23.9	18.2	15.6	18.9
best machine learning course	18.6	19.6	19.4	17.1	15.0	16.4	21.4	26.0	26.1	22.5	19.6
artificial intelligence books	21.1	12.1	7.5	9.9	16.2	20.4	20.2	18.4	19.2	22.7	24.9
best data science courses	23.3	19.3	16.3	15.7	16.8	17.7	17.5	17.1	17.8	19.1	19.0
data science classes	16.9	18.9	20.3	19.9	17.7	15.4	14.6	15.7	17.1	17.5	17.0
data science pdf	10.0	14.9	19.7	21.0	18.7	15.7	15.0	16.8	18.5	18.0	16.2
data science book	9.0	11.8	14.7	15.5	14.4	13.4	13.7	14.6	14.5	13.3	12.3
best data science course	12.4	13.8	13.9	12.2	9.9	8.6	8.4	8.8	9.1	9.5	10.6
ai book	8.6	8.7	10.4	12.0	12.0	10.7	9.9	10.5	12.1	13.1	12.4
best machine learning book	8.3	6.7	8.6	12.9	16.9	18.2	15.6	10.0	3.9	0.6	2.1
machine learning classes	9.6	11.8	13.2	12.9	11.8	11.2	11.4	11.1	9.5	7.4	6.5

Based on the analysis above, the time people care about data science courses in the first few weeks of 2021 will be the week of January 17, 2021. For people searching for AI and machine learning books, it's a couple weeks later, the week of January 31, 2021.

As I write this in the last week of December 2020, I need to put together a marketing plan for releasing this book at the end of January, in about a month's time. Suddenly, instead of guessing when I should release my book, I have a clear target date that aligns with when audiences should have peak interest in the book based on what they're likely to be searching for.

From this insight, I'll need to build a marketing operations calendar - social posts, emails, maybe even some ads - to help boost the awareness of the book in the next couple of weeks. That way, just as audience interest begins to increase, I'll be present and visible.

Let's dig down one more step, to the individual words and phrases themselves.

* * *

Topics to Create Content for Week Of 2021-01-17

term	importance
data science course	1
data science classes	2
data science pdf	3
machine learning pdf	4
machine learning courses	5

Topics to Create Content for Week Of 2021-01-24

term	importance
machine learning pdf	1
data science pdf	2
data science classes	3
machine learning book	4
data science book	5

Topics to Create Content for Week Of 2021-01-31

term	importance
machine learning pdf	1
data science pdf	2
machine learning book	3
machine learning books	4
best machine learning book	5

We take the data and split it out into a weekly

calendar. If I want to be aligned with the audience searching for all these topics, then each week, I should be creating some content that goes after these search terms - along with paid search ads targeting these terms - to maximize the chances that people will find my book relevant during when they're most interested in the overall topic. Maybe have a series of blog posts, or newsletter articles, social posts, some YouTube videos that are topically-optimized so that anyone searching for these particular phrases within the topic finds my stuff.

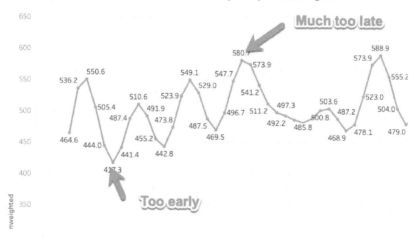

VIsualized Content Predictions 2021 : Analysis by TrustInsights.ai

In the example above, for people searching for a data science course, there are clearly periods of time throughout the first half of 2021 which are better or worse. The week of February 7 is probably the worst time to be in market - people aren't looking nearly as much. But rolling out our marketing the week of May 23 is much too late - we've missed several early opportunities and we'd just be ramping up our spend and activity as interest goes into a sustained decline.

Imagine using the same techniques for your marketing. When will certain ideas or topics trend? Not just in general - we all know the broad generalities of a cyclical topic - but the specifics. What exact week of the year should we have our marketing content and tactics in motion to maximize the opportunity?

This is the power of effective forecasting - to know with granularity and accuracy what's likely to happen. When we combine machine learning tools, domain expertise, and experience, we significantly improve the likelihood that our marketing will resonate with our audiences.

Problem 5: Marketing to the unknown

Despite the machines being intermediaries for what content gets to our audiences, machines aren't the ultimate end customer. The end customer is still the human, the person who has to make a decision about what to buy and who to buy from. To reach that person, we have to navigate a complicated web of interactions, from reviews to referrals to conversations.

We intuitively understand the idea of a personal network. We each have our circles of friends - work friends, social friends, hobby friends - and we intuitively understand that we make decisions based on the information from those networks every day. We ask our friends for recommendations, either publicly or privately. We read reviews and ask opinions from both friends and total strangers. We watch videos of unboxing and how-to on YouTube, follow our favorite prominent figures on Instagram, have conversations on Twitter and in networks like Slack and Discord.

The challenge for us as marketers is bringing

order and structure to these very disorderly interactions so that we can make informed choices about where to focus our time and effort. Do we find a big name influencer to build awareness of our product? Do we find a private community to share and discuss our services? How do we navigate these networks?

A machine learning technology known as network graphing does exactly this. Given a list of interactions, network graphing helps draw the literal network connecting people together. Here's a simplified example of how it works.

Suppose we have four people, Ianis, Zohaib, Kirstin, and Mahnoor. On Instagram, Kirstin posts a photo challenge to her friends. Zohaib and Mahnoor participate, tagging Kirstin in their photos. Ianis sees Zohaib's post and creates one of their own, tagging in Zohaib. We end up with this set of interactions:

* * *

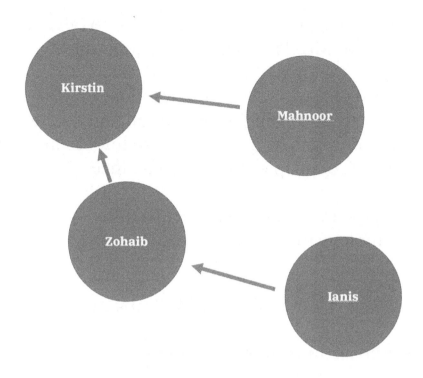

That's the essence of a network graph. By diagramming out the connections between entities - Instagram users in this case - we visualize and understand who's important to a network. If we wanted to reach out to this community, who would be the logical person to contact if we wanted to reach as many people as possible? Kirstin, of course, in this example. She's the person that all the interactions flow towards.

When we're dealing with just a handful of people, mapping out interactions like this is very straightforward. But when we're talking about hundreds, thousands, or millions of people, the data becomes instantly overwhelming. There's no practical way to draw out every single connection and do the kinds of organizing necessary to understand a network of people without assistance.

Let's explore how we might use this technology in a walkthrough.

Network Graphing Walkthrough

Suppose, for example, we wanted to understand the network around people on Instagram using the black-owned small business hashtags #blackbusiness and #blackowned. How much data are we talking about? Millions and millions of posts.

* * *

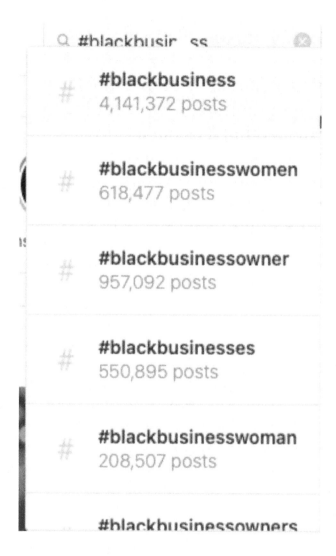

Downloading even just a subset of these
results is still hundreds of thousands of posts.
Using Facebook's Crowdtangle software
(which provides historical Facebook,
Instagram, and Reddit data), #BlackBusiness
and #BlackOwned for just 2020 return a

sample of 151,139 unique, distinct posts.

The only way to make sense of this much data is to use network graphing. After cleaning up the data and inspecting it to make sure it's coherent, we visualize it with a more complex version of the example network graph, looking at who's being mentioned the most in the #BlackBusiness and #BlackOwned hashtags:

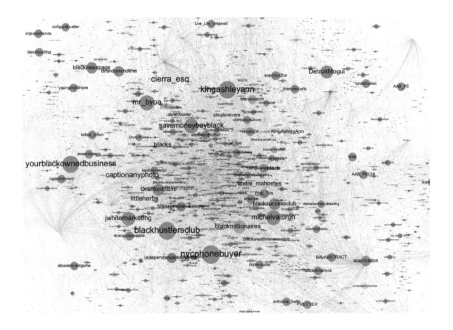

While complex to look at, it's functionally no different than our example with Kirstin and company. What do we see in this graph? The bigger the bubble, the more people who have talked about/tagged that account - these are the accounts most talked about.

Contrast that with how marketers typically do influencer identification. They'll look at data like who's got the biggest number of followers, or who has the highest engagement rates. These are fairly primitive ways to measure influence, especially since they're not especially meaningful. Combining network graphing with natural language processing (from Problem 3) would allow even further refinement of people talking about just a topic we care about.

What's even more interesting is that when we compare our influence score based on being most talked about to these more common measures, we find that there isn't a strong correlation - the most talked about accounts aren't necessarily the ones with the biggest followings:

* * *

user_name	influencesco	community	degree	indegree	outdegree	followers
nycphonebuyer	1	0	14	13	1	8668
blackhustlersclub	0.969181	0	22	19	3	206897
kingashleyann	0.947946	0	14	13	1	293647
yourblackownedbusiness	0.924486	0	14	13	1	48990
cierra_esq	0.909772	16	17	17	0	37685
soproud2beblack	0.841696	0	120	12	108	69724
savemoneybuyblack	0.804248	0	17	10	7	31529
jwhitemarketing	0.743365	0	37	7	30	7393
blackmillionaires_	0.700805	58	59	13	46	183920
blacks	0.692105	30	17	17	0	1528
black	0.597693	16	16	16	0	730411
tallguytycoon	0.585096	120	7	7	0	110311
staccnation	0.546859	0	156	6	150	49375
shoplovevera	0.507196	16	14	13	1	170150
blackrealestatedialogue	0.499364	195	31	7	24	9971
blackwealthrenaissance	0.484502	27	20	13	7	316411
drangelaspeaks	0.47431	0	3	3	0	3920
blocalsearch	0.467414	58	37	5	32	13526
10thpowaproducts	0.466859	0	8	6	2	9769
melaninindex	0.456006	0	225	3	222	14612

What happens when we focus on these most-connected accounts, rather than the biggest audiences? We end up focusing on the tastemakers, the people who are true opinion leaders, trendsetters - exactly the kind of person or organization we'd love to have representing our products. Why? Because they don't necessarily have the biggest audiences, they may cost less than reaching out to, say, a Kardashian but still be able to get our products and services in front of a massive audience, thanks to how interconnected they are.

Going back to our earlier example, imagine if our accounts looked like this, where the bubble size represented the number of followers:

* * *

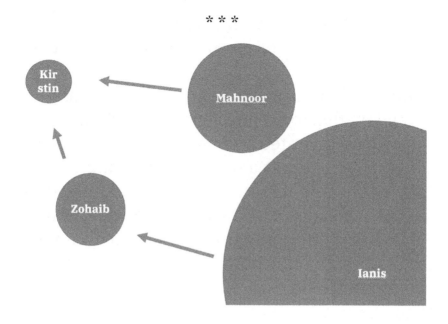

In this example, if we tried to reach out to Ianis with a gazillion followers, he might say, "Sure, it'll be $140,000 for me to share 2 pictures on my Instagram account". We might not have that much budget. But if we reached out to Kirstin, she might say, "Sure, I'll take a free product and $250" - and yet, if we know she's a tastemaker, our product or service might reach Ianis' desk for free AND be more credible because it's not coming from us - it's coming from Kirstin via Zohaib.

That's the power of network graphing - the ability to reach into networks and diagram them out, understand who the players are, and then strategically work with those networks to find the best fits for our budget and resources.

Network graphing applies to more than just social media, too. The original PageRank algorithm invented by Sergey Brin and Larry Page at Google was a network graphing algorithm, and the graph of inbound links that forms the basis of SEO is still a network graph at its heart. We could use the same techniques to understand link communities in our areas of interest.

Network graphing can even be used in more traditional forms of identification, such as academic papers. In nearly every academic paper, we'll find a list of citations, either in the footnotes or at the end of the paper:

REFERENCES

[1] ABADI, M., AGARWAL, A., BARHAM, P., BREVDO, E., CHEN, Z., CITRO, C., CORRADO, G. S., DAVIS, A., DEAN, J., DEVIN, M., GHEMAWAT, S., GOODFELLOW, I., HARP, A., IRVING, G., ISARD, M., JIA, Y., JOZEFOWICZ, R., KAISER, L., KUDLUR, M., LEVENBERG, J., MANÉ, D., MONGA, R., MOORE, S., MURRAY, D., OLAH, C., SCHUSTER, M., SHLENS, J., STEINER, B., SUTSKEVER, I., TALWAR, K., TUCKER, P., VANHOUCKE, V., VASUDEVAN, V., VIÉGAS, F., VINYALS, O., WARDEN, P., WATTENBERG, M., WICKE, M., YU, Y., AND ZHENG, X. TensorFlow: Large-scale machine learning on heterogeneous systems, 2015. Software available from tensorflow.org.

[2] ABRAMS, S., WAMBUA, J., SANTERMANS, E., WILLEM, L., KUYLEN, E., COLETTI, P., LIBIN, P., FAES, C., PETROF, O., HERZOG, S. A., BEUTELS, P., AND HENS, N. Modeling the early phase of the belgian covid-19 epidemic using a stochastic compartmental model and studying its implied future trajectories. *medRxiv* (2020).

[3] BEAUMONT, M. A. Approximate bayesian computation in evolution and ecology. *Annual review of ecology, evolution, and systematics 41* (2010), 379–406.

[4] BROWN, G. D., OLESON, J. J., AND PORTER, A. T. An empirically adjusted approach to reproductive number estimation for stochastic compartmental models: A case study of two ebola outbreaks. *Biometrics 72*, 2 (2016), 335–343.

[5] CALVET, L. E., AND CZELLAR, V. Accurate methods for approximate bayesian computation filtering. *Journal of Financial Econometrics 13*, 4 (2015), 798–838.

[6] DONG, E., DU, H., AND GARDNER, L. An interactive web-based dashboard to track COVID-19 in real time, vol. 20. Lancet Publishing Group, may 2020.

[7] DROVANDI, C. C., AND PETTITT, A. N. Estimation of Parameters for Macroparasite Population Evolution Using Approximate Bayesian Computation. *Biometrics 67*, 1 (mar 2011), 225–233.

[8] DUTTA, R., SCHOENGENS, M., PACCHIARDI, L., UMMADISINGU, A., WIDMER, N., ONNELA, J.-P., AND MIRA, A. Abcpy: A high-performance computing perspective to approximate

We would use the exact same network graphing technology to understand who is the most cited in academic papers, creating a network graph for our topic of interest. This is especially powerful in fields where influencers might not be active on traditional social networks, or where network data isn't available, such as cybersecurity. Plenty of people in cybersecurity have no interest whatsoever in being publicly visible in places like Facebook, which they regard as fundamental threats to privacy and data security. Yet if we want to understand who's who, these same individuals will be principal investigators or project leaders in academic papers on cutting-edge computer security topics, and we could just as easily identify them by citations.

Any time we've got a collection of data that represents interactions between entities, be they people, organizations, or content, we have the opportunity to use network graphing to distill down the data into something comprehensible, something we can take action on.

The Journey to AI

So, we know the practical applications of AI when it comes to marketing and some key techniques. That's like knowing that recipes exist for the dishes you want to cook. How do you make the leap from recipe to meal?

The process of becoming an AI-first company isn't fast or easy. It's a seven-step journey that many organizations will undertake at some point. The first four steps are mandatory for every company, regardless of type or industry. The last few steps will be taken by those whose core competency will be heavily influenced by AI. Let's take a moment to unpack that before moving into the journey itself.

Build or Buy?

One of the questions I'm asked most about the use of AI and machine learning in marketing is the question of whether to buy or build - whether to develop in-house capabilities, or seek out a vendor/partner to use their capabilities instead.

The knee jerk answer to this question is

straightforward, and depends on what you've got more of: time or money. If you've got more money than time, buy it; if you've got more time than money, build it.

While that's a helpful rule of thumb, it ignores a key consideration: **strategy.**

What's your organization's digital strategy? Right now, one of the most buzzy buzzwords in business strategy is *digital transformation,* which is a catch-all term for companies trying to be digital-first. Lots of companies, especially in 2020, got to experience digital transformation at a breakneck pace as the pandemic forced offline companies to go online, forced the physical into the virtual.

At its heart, digital transformation means your strategic choices revolve around being digital first, instead of shoe-horning digital processes and technologies onto traditional business. Digital-first means you recognize the value of the data you're creating with your digital products, services, and processes.

This means that instead of being a cost center, companies which have digitally transformed have figured out **how to make money on their**

data, the analysis of their data, and critically, machine learning models which are built on their data.

The textbook example of this strategy predates commercial AI by a number of years. Back in the late 20th century, American Airlines built a reservation booking system that powered its passenger reservations. It was a world-class system known as SABRE, and it was so good at what it did that other airlines asked to use it. SABRE became the industry standard - and a lucrative source of revenue for American Airlines that required no additional airplanes. They figured out how to make a system built on their data highly profitable.

This is what it means to be digitally transformed: **you've figured out how to build new products and services based on your data.**

How might this play out?

Let's say you're a music school that gives private lessons to kids. During the pandemic, you had to shut down your physical building for safety reasons, and all your teachers and students went on Zoom. That isn't digital transformation in and of itself, it's just applying digital technologies to a traditional process. But now, let's say you've started recording all your Zoom classes and suddenly you have a huge course catalog of pre-recorded Zoom classes. Instead of business as usual, you open up a virtual school where students can consume the recordings at one price point or get the experience of a live teacher at a higher price point. You're now leveraging your data - making use of your data - as its own line of business. That's a true digital transformation.

Now, for a more complex example related to machine learning, suppose you were a coffee growing company whose chief product was coffee beans. As part of the effort to grow better and higher yields, you used data, analytics, and machine learning to understand and predict what makes for the healthiest, most productive coffee trees. You collected data on soil nutrients, water, sunshine, air quality, altitude, insects, diseases, the works. Everything you could gather to improve your understanding of how to grow coffee beans.

Suppose you took that understanding and applied the various machine learning techniques we discussed previously to the data. You build a series of algorithms and techniques which accurately predict how well your coffee is going to do. You could stop there and be a very profitable coffee plantation.

But, if you're a digitally transformed coffee plantation, you could do more. You'd keep cranking out great coffee, because that's your core competency. But what if you picked up that model and changed the input data from coffee trees to corn stalks? You could make a second line of business providing your AI-powered model to companies growing all sorts of things. That's a digital transformation with machine learning and AI, where your software - the model - can be reused for more than one purpose and is a line of revenue by itself.

Which brings us back to the question of "build or buy?" The answer depends on whether or not your applications of machine learning are central to your core competency. If, as in the coffee tree example above, we are applying machine learning to the core competency of your company, it would be foolish to buy AI from a vendor. You have less control over the model and almost no control what a vendor does with the model - including licensing it to your competitors. When machine learning is successfully applied to your core competency, it becomes part of your secret sauce, and that's not something you should give up control over lightly. You should only buy it in that situation if you simply cannot afford to build the technology yourself.

On the other hand, if you're applying machine learning to non-core functions - for example, if the coffee company were using machine learning to improve its SEO - then buying from a vendor is perfectly fine. You want to reserve any serious machine learning budget or people for improving your core competency. Better to select vendors for non-core competencies who are best in class, who have figured out how to apply machine learning to their core competencies instead.

Why does this matter? The journey to AI is a journey that can take between four and seven steps. Depending on whether you are applying it to a core competency versus just improving business operations determines which path you'll take.

* * *

The Enterprise AI Journey

AI-Powered	AI across the enterprise and in every relevant role
Machine Learning	Advancing process automation and data science with supervised, unsupervised, reinforcement learning
Data Science	Exploring the unknowns, building statistical and math capabilities, code and engineering
Process Automation	Automating the known knowns, finding efficiencies, scaling processes
Insights & Research	Qualitative capabilities, explaining the data story, market research
Measurement & Analytics	Becoming data-driven, identifying and measuring KPIs, understanding what happened
Data Foundation	Finding, cleaning, preparing, and unifying enterprise data sources

Copyright © 2021 Christopher S. Penn | @cspenn | cspenn.com | @trustinsights | TrustInsights.ai

The Journey to AI, Step 1: Data

The journey to AI unsurprisingly begins with data. Since machine learning software trains on data, it's the most important foundational element to making machine learning work for your organization. What data do you have? As we covered data quality in the chapter on data, we won't rehash it here.

What's paramount to machine learning, and to our journey to AI, is that we be able to speak to our data capabilities thoroughly. In the technology world, this is known as systems architecture, and it's something marketers have not had to learn until now. Consider the key questions we should ask of every piece of data we're considering using for machine learning:

- Who has responsibility for the data?
- What data do we have within our organization?
- Where does all our data live?
- When was our data collected?
- Why do we have or lack certain data?
- How do we collect and store data?

Without proper processes and governance of our data, our machine learning efforts will be stymied. We must have a firm foundation based on data before anything else.

This point, by the way, is where most companies are stopped in their tracks by their machine learning aspirations. If data is our key ingredient, then most companies have either empty pantries or pantries full of rotted food - and in either situation, you can't cook.

The Journey to AI, Step 2: Analytics
***

The second step in our AI journey is developing our analytics capabilities. Can we answer the question, using our current data and methods, of what happened?

When we look at our data, what happened?

Do we have goals that we measure towards?

Do we have key performance indicators which tell us our progress towards our goals?

Analytics capabilities mean we have the ability to answer basic questions about our data, and without these capabilities, we cannot make effective use of machine learning. We'll forever be just dabbling, experimenting, tinkering without an objective or outcome. While that's fun, that's not going to pay the bills for our department, our company.

Consider one of the most popular applications of machine learning that the average consumer uses frequently: the maps app on your smartphone. It's got incredible power, to understand a route, re-route in case of trouble, and help you make the most of your journey.

But that app is useless if you don't put in a

destination.

The same is true for your machine learning efforts. No amount of machine learning power will help you if you don't have the basics of analytics in place.

Becoming data-driven is also not a technology problem, nor is it something you can solve with technology. It's principally a people problem - a cultural shift inside your organization. Being data-driven means making decisions with data first, as opposed to taking data into consideration but then falling back to old habits like experience, intuition, or emotion. If you can't make data-driven decisions with the data you already have, then you won't accept the outputs of machine learning - and thus any machine learning initiative is ultimately doomed.

The Journey to AI, Step 3: Insights

The third step in our AI journey is developing our qualitative capabilities. When it comes to understanding our data, analytics is all about answering the key question of what happened?

What's not possible with analytics is the ability

to answer why. Website traffic was up 40% yesterday. Okay... why? Our rankings have dropped by 15% on Bing. Why?

The more complex the data, the more difficult it is to answer why, unless you have qualitative data capabilities, which can include:

- Customer advisory boards
- Focus groups
- Surveys
- Interviews
- Shop-alongs
- In-place video observation
- Lifestyle immersion
- Journals/diaries

These methods all help us understand why our data says what it says in ways that quantitative analysis alone cannot. As amazing as AI is, no machine can climb inside our heads and understand what we're thinking, why we make the choices we make.

We need qualitative abilities, especially when we work with unstructured data (like in text mining) so that we can apply best practices and rigor to our efforts. Without a solid foundation in qualitative research, we cannot shed light on our quantitative data. When we embark on machine learning techniques with unstructured data, we equally risk misinterpreting or building flawed models without that qualitative foundation.

The Journey to AI, Step 4: Process Automation

The fourth step in our AI journey is building a discipline of process automation. This may or may not involve machine learning later on, but process automation brings two benefits to organizations: scale and quality.

What is process automation? It's exactly as it sounds in name - a concerted effort to automate as many tasks or processes as possible to find efficiencies and free up time and resources in your organization.

Process automation always begins with process documentation and governance. We can't automate what we don't know. By documenting processes using many of the same methods as used in qualitative research, we build a deep understanding of how work is done within our organization.

* * *

Once we know the recipes for achieving work, we can look to improve them. If we have, for example, five employees in a customer service department, and one of them is substantially more productive than the others, we can look at the winning employee's processes and apply them to the rest of the staff.

After documentation, we begin the work of automation, using technology to augment or take over the most repetitive, mundane tasks. This can be as simple as a library of macros for common tasks in our office software, or as complex as what's called *robotic process automation* in which a computer records our movements on-screen and plays them back.

For example, suppose you post content on social media every day. What's the process, the general recipe for doing so? It probably looks something like this:

- Source text and images
- Craft post drafts in a CMS or spreadsheet
- Receive approvals for drafted content
- Copy and paste text content into the scheduling tool
- Load images or multimedia into the scheduling tool

- Set post dates and times
- Set post tracking codes
- Verify that the posts published correctly on the assigned dates and times
- Review the analytics and performance of the posts

Each stage of this process has opportunities for automation, for reducing the amount of time that it takes to do something. Any time you see "copy and paste" in documentation of a process, you know for sure the process has easy automation opportunities.

Process automation creates scale in the same way a cooking recipe brings scale. Once documented, the recipe can be shared with other chefs, so that many can make a dish instead of just one person.

Process automation also brings quality in the same way as a cooking recipe. Once documented, a recipe has a set list of ingredients and directions that allow someone else to replicate the result with a minimum of errors and deviations from the standard. That standardization means quality can continuously improve over time, instead of restarting from scratch every time.

* * *

Decision Time

At this point in the AI journey, we must determine if we're applying AI to a core competency or not. If we're not, at this point in our journey we are well-prepared to engage with a vendor and use their best-in-class software, models, and techniques to empower our existing data, analytics, research, and automation efforts. Everything we've learned up to this point is ideal for us to evaluate vendors and understand whether they know what they're talking about or not, whether they're using AI - and what - in their product or service.

If we're applying AI to our core competency, then this is the point where we start building serious in-house capabilities - at serious investments of time, money, and people. We'll need them in order to build and maintain our secret sauce - machine learning-powered core competency.

What are those next steps?

The Journey to AI, Step 5: Data Science Capabilities

*** *** ***

The fifth step in the journey to AI, and the first step for those companies in which AI will be part of the core competency, is to develop robust data science capabilities.

Undoubtedly, you've heard the term data science or data scientist frequently in recent times. What does it mean? The generally-accepted definition, via Wikipedia, is:

"Data science is an interdisciplinary field that uses scientific methods, processes, algorithms and systems to extract knowledge and insights from data in various forms, both structured and unstructured, similar to data mining."

That's not super helpful, so instead, let's look at this definition from Dr. Hal Varian:

"The ability to take data — to be able to understand it, to process it, to extract value from it, to visualize it, to communicate it — that's going to be a hugely important skill in the next decades." - Hal Varian, chief economist at Google and UC Berkeley professor of information sciences, business, and economics

That's a much more robust definition. However, there's a key part missing, which

Wikipedia does note - the scientific method. Let's create a merged definition.

Data science is the process of understanding, processing, extracting value from, visualizing, and communicating data using the scientific method.

The scientific method is critical to our understanding of data science; without it, we're just hacking away randomly at data. Any value we deliver will be purely by luck instead of using rigorous, well-defined processes that create repeatable results. Implicit in the scientific method are also concepts like ethics and experimentation; in data science, we're not seeking to make the known better as much as we are seeking to make the unknown known.

This is also what differentiates data science from things like analytics, which is step 2 of the journey to AI. However, the skills that make for great analytics capabilities are transferable to data science, as are the skills that make for great qualitative analysis in step 3 of the journey to AI. In data science, we extend those capabilities with two key skill sets.

* * *

Analytics and qualitative research demand business and domain **expertise**. You need to understand what's going on and your field/industry well enough to create informed, quality research. Data science adds the necessary skills of **technical development** (programming) and **statistical/mathematical** understanding. Top data scientists - and there are precious few of them - are proficient in each area: **business**, **programming**, and **mathematics**.

Data science, then, is not just a profession of its own, but a meta-profession of skills rolled up into one or several individuals. A true data scientist has some capability in each of the three areas of statistics, programming, and business.

When we talk about the journey to AI and building AI capabilities in-house, the data scientist will be one of the principals spearheading the effort. They'll be constructing models, validating data, tuning the cleaning methods, building data pipelines, and running many, many experiments in the lab to advance your data capabilities.

* * *

To extend our cooking analogies, data science is the recipe construction department, your test kitchen. Up until this step in your journey, you've been getting all the ingredients sourced and ready. Process automation helped you write down the recipes you know, and now data science will help you tweak, experiment, and improve your recipes. You're experimenting a lot until you find the winning recipes for your business and your data.

Data science and machine learning are not one and the same, but it's fair to say that without data science, there can be no machine learning of any quality. Data science can provide tremendous value to an organization by itself, without machine learning, but it becomes a powerhouse when paired with machine learning.

A Brief Word on Talent Quality

One of the recent phenomena to crop up is the number of universities and companies offering courses and certifications like "Crash Course in Data Science" and "Become a Data Scientist in 6 Weeks" bootcamps, intensives, etc.

* * *

Given that we've just outlined that data science itself is a profession composed of other professions, the idea that someone can become a data scientist in six weeks is ludicrous.

Imagine that same offering applied to any other rigorous profession and see how silly it sounds. Would you really go to someone who had a "Six Week Crash Course in Neurosurgery" and no other medical qualifications? I certainly wouldn't. So, buyer beware: a reputable data scientist requires either proper academic credentials (typically in mathematics) or extensive field experience and training. Just as a test kitchen requires a master chef, so your data science efforts require a master data scientist.

The Journey to AI, Step 6: Machine Learning Capabilities

After building data science capabilities, the next step in the journey is to elevate them using machine learning. If data science is the process of creating the best recipes possible using programming, statistics, and business expertise, then this stage in our journey is about taking those recipes and putting them into production.

To return to the cooking analogy, when our recipe leaves the test kitchen, we have to scale it up to be served at all our restaurants.

Because machine learning today is reliant on technical expertise, at this point in the journey, your data science team will be collaborating with your IT teams to bring the recipes, the proofs of concept, the small-scale pilot projects to life. Much of the code, technical architecture, and requirements are already known because you defined them during the data science phase of the journey. Now, IT will be operationalizing those smaller projects for rollout.

At this stage in the journey, if you're building AI capabilities into your marketing because marketing is a core competency, you'll likely be involved as a domain expert for marketing knowledge, but you will not be doing any of the implementation. Your primary role will be in validating the outcomes from your machine learning implementations, helping IT and your data science team quality-check the results.

* * *

The Journey To AI, Step 7: AI-Powered

The first machine learning project to successfully deploy within an organization is always a long slog to victory. It takes a significant amount of time, effort, people, and budget to bring a project to fruition around anything that's a core competency of the organization, because the stakes are so high.

However, once the first project is done successfully, it paves the way for future projects until your leadership eventually adopts a "How can we apply AI to X" for everything in the company. That's when you've completed the journey to AI, when it becomes a company-wide strategic imperative.

Today, there are only a handful of companies that have achieved that level of success with AI that makes it a strategic mandate. Companies like IBM, Google, Microsoft, Facebook, Amazon, and Apple have made the leap to using machine learning whenever and wherever possible in their core competencies.

It's important to note that not every company needs to embrace AI as fully as these big technology companies have. However, if better, faster, and cheaper are mandates you face in your company, AI is a likely solution to at least some of those woes. Go the vendor route after step 4 in the journey if it's not impacting a core competency, and take the rest of the journey after step 4 if you need to vastly improve your core competency.

As with any journey, we need to make preparations before we set out. Next, we'll look at what it will take to prepare your company for the journey.

Preparing Your Company For AI

You're about to set out on a journey. What do you do to prepare? You make sure you have a destination, maps, and supplies. We've talked about the destination (analytics, goals, KPIs) and maps (the Journey to AI). Let's talk about supplies next, in terms of people and technology.

I'm a big fan of Dr. Clive Humby's expression that "data is the new oil", from 2006. If you've ever seen or touched crude oil, you know it to be a disgusting, goopy, sticky mess that stains everything it touches, burns with an acrid smoke, and is almost completely useless in its raw state. In order to create value from oil, we need to extract it from the ground, refine it, and then bring the refined products to market, to people who can use them.

Data is much the same. In its raw state, locked away in proprietary applications, siloed databases, vendor walls, and departmental politics, data is more hazard than benefit. Untouched, data is a cost - a cost for computer space to house it, a cost for people to maintain it, and a massive cost if it contains sensitive, personally-identifying information (which many marketing databases do). The only place where the analogy to oil breaks down is that data isn't consumed when used.

To make data useful, we look to the steps needed in the journey to AI - the ability to identify it, extract it from the places it's stored, refine it with process automation and data science, and deploy it in production using machine learning and line of business applications.

In order to accomplish this, we'll need two things: people and process. Just as one does not simply dig a hole in the ground and immediately benefit from oil, neither does a company simply sit down one day and say, "okay, we're using our data now!". At least, not if the company wants to be successful.

So, who are the people and what is the process?

The People Your Company Needs

If we think about the process of extraction, transformation, and bringing to market data (or oil), we need people who can extract the resource, refine the resource, and then transport and ultimately use the resource.

When it comes to data extraction, we'll need two types of people: **developers** and **data architects**.

Developers will be the people writing code and connecting to the data wherever it lives in our company. This is no small undertaking; for large, distributed companies, just the process alone of finding the data can be a mammoth undertaking. The older a company is, the more likely that company has incurred what's called technical debt, inheriting legacy systems (and legacy data) that makes extraction difficult.

Data architects are the people who work alongside the developers to capture the raw data as they extract it from systems and store it somewhere for further use. If developers are the oil well drillers, data architects are the truck and tanker captains moving the raw data around safely.

Once the raw data has been extracted, we need to refine it - clean it, prepare it, follow all the steps we covered in the 6C framework for data quality. This task, as we saw in the previous chapter, is the domain of the **data scientist**. We'll need data scientists to refine and transform the data into data products: analysis, insights, models, dashboards, visualizations, etc. - everything we'd need to make use of the data. In our oil analogy, these are the refineries that turn crude petroleum into everything from gasoline to plastics.

After refining, our data products need to be brought to our users. Data products are of no use if they simply sit on a server or in a drawer, never used. Remember at the beginning of the book, we reviewed the appalling fact that 63% of CMOs do not use analytics in the decision-making process? This is the role of the **marketing technologist**, the person who speaks both the language of data products and the language of marketing, who takes the data products and helps business users make the most of them.

Marketing technologists often are the folks working in marketing operations, helping make the most of technologies like marketing automation and CRM systems, so it makes logical sense that the use of data products would fall to them. They'd be best suited to help introduce data products into existing processes and workflows.

So, that's the roster of who you'll need to make AI work for you; if your company is pursuing AI as a core competency, you'll need all four roles. If you're not pursuing it as a core competency booster, then you'll need marketing technologists the most, to help you effectively evaluate vendors and determine who's the real deal.

That's the people resources you'll need. What about process?

The Process Blueprint

The journey to AI, which we discussed previously, lays out the conceptual steps you'll take to reach your AI destination. However, the journey is a meta-process that incorporates many other steps. Given the importance of the marketing technologist for non-core competency implementations and the shared responsibility among developers and data scientists for core competency implementations, it's necessary for us to examine governance.

* * *

By governance, I mean a blueprint for how all the components and pieces of the journey to AI are monitored, measured, and managed. Our compatriots in IT have had governance processes and procedures for decades. As primarily a cost center, IT has had to demonstrate efficiency and effectiveness time and again to justify maintaining or increasing technology expenditures.

Marketing technology has reached this level of scrutiny in many organizations. Marketers have spent the last decade going hog-wild, buying dozens of point solutions to solve specific marketing problems, but in doing so creating technological chaos that makes the journey to AI more difficult than it should be.

So, what can marketers borrow from IT to bring the same levels of discipline to marketing technology? The single best answer is a governance framework.

For close to 30 years, IT has governed and managed itself through an internationally-accepted framework, the ISO 38500 framework for governance. This framework lays out at a strategic level everything a Chief Information Officer or Chief Technology

Officer needs to consider and have under their watchful eye in order to be successful. When consulting firms perform an audit of a company, it's this type of framework that's used to validate a company's internal alignment.

Marketing technology can adopt this framework wholesale. In fact, at Trust Insights, we strongly recommend that you do. Let's dig into it.

The Trust Insights MarTech / AI Governance Framework (ISO 38500-2015)

Concept	Function	Application	Measurement
Responsibility	Business Strategy	Models, Environment, Strategies	Business Metrics, Plans, Balanced Scorecard, P&L
Strategy	MarTech Strategy	MT Strategy, Architecture, Principles	Zachman Framework, Balanced Scorecard, Marketing P&L
Acquisition	MT Balance Sheet	Capital, Data, Applications, Processes, Technologies, IP	Patents, IP, IC/ICR
Performance	MT Operations	MarkOps, MT Ops, Asset Management, Security	TCO/ROI, ISO 27001, 6 Sigma
Conformance	Risk & Compliance	Governance, Conformance, Compliance, Risk Management, Controls, Audits	CoBIT, SOX, PCI DSS, ISO 27001, ISO 38500
Humanity	Change Management	Project Management, Methods, Alignment, Training	PM, Capability Maturity Model Integration

The ISO 38500 framework, as modified for marketing technology, encompasses the same six broad concepts:

* * *

- Responsibility: how technology serves the overall mandates of the business
- Strategy: the technical strategy itself
- Acquisition: the financial aspects of technology
- Performance: the operational aspects of technology
- Conformance: the legal and risk management of technology
- Humanity: the interface between technology and people

Each conceptual area of the framework then has a specific interdepartmental function, applications of that function within the business, and measurement methods. Let's unpack each of these.

Within **responsibility** is **business strategy**.

What are the overall models, strategies, and the business environment that provide context for technology choices? Business strategy must dictate the application of technology, not the other way around.

The responsibility portion of a marketing technology audit must be done first and foremost, to ensure everything else is aligned with the business strategy.

When we measure business strategy's impact, we measure on key business performance indicators such as profit and loss, revenue, etc.

Within **strategy** is **marketing technology strategy**.

What is the overall marketing technology strategy? Examples would be something like an AI-first strategy, or a cloud computing strategy, something that dictates what all major choices must be weighed against. There can even be specific vendor requirements as part of the marketing technology strategy; if a company uses SAP for its enterprise resource planning, in theory there should be additional benefits to using SAP for marketing technology.

In addition to marketing technology strategy, this layer of the framework also includes overall marketing strategy. Is the overall marketing strategy aligned with marketing technology strategy? For example, if our overall strategy is weighted towards customer retention, but all our technology spend is going to acquisition, then we have a strategic mismatch.

This layer of the framework is measured in things like the Zachman Framework, balanced scorecards, or more commonly, the overall KPIs of marketing. Is marketing hitting its numbers?

Within **acquisition** is the **marketing technology balance sheet**.

This stage is one of the most overlooked in marketing generally, but especially as companies make the journey to AI. The balance sheet is everything of value that marketing technology is producing. This includes data, intellectual property (IP), technology, models, processes, and capital.

When we were examining the journey to AI, we looked at whether AI was going to be part of the core competency or not. This layer, the balance sheet, is essential to any company applying AI to its core competency, because the balance sheet is where we track the value of AI's benefits. In the example of growing coffee trees, the machine learning model's value (and applicability to other crops) would be tracked on the balance sheet like any other asset.

What assets and value does marketing create? Even something as simple as storing photos for marketing collateral would belong here. Your employees' stock photos that they take with their smartphones and contribute to the company newsletter have value as intellectual property. Anyone who believes photos and media don't have value has never been sued by Getty Images.

That's the acid test for intellectual property; as you audit your marketing and technology, ask the simple question: *if we were caught using someone else's intellectual property (for whatever process you're auditing) would we lose a lawsuit?* If the answer is yes, then tracking that IP, that data, that software, those processes is part of the balance sheet. It almost goes without saying that everything you do in data science and machine learning, every method, every line of code belongs on the balance sheet.

The balance sheet itself is a tracking mechanism, but so are more formal methods of tracking IP such as patent grants, copyright applications, and other paperwork that proves the data products you're creating are worth protecting.

Within performance is marketing technology operations.

In the journey to AI, the fourth stage was all about process automation. When we audit our marketing technology and our marketing operations, we're examining and documenting those processes in detail. Marketing technology operations is all about overall marketing operations, technology-specific marketing operations, asset management, security, and the execution of marketing.

When we audit marketing technology operations, we're really looking for that process documentation and process management. How thorough are we in our understanding of how marketing works within our organization?

Measuring marketing operations is straightforward; we use the same measurements as any operational function in a company. This could be ROI, total cost of ownership, or more formal project and process management methodologies like 6

Sigma.

Within **conformance** is **risk and compliance management**.

This is the part of a governance audit that almost everyone universally dislikes. Risk and compliance management is all about governance, conformance to stated policies, processes, and procedures, risk management, controls, and audits. In short, it's the mitigation or elimination of controllable risks within a company's marketing technology.

While few people enjoy risk and compliance management, it's become an essential part of modern marketing technology, and one which will take an increasingly large amount of focus and resources in the years to come. A relatively contemporary example of this as it impacts marketing was the rollout and enforcement of the EU General Data Protection Regulation, or GDPR. Marketers had to scramble to achieve and maintain compliance, lest their companies be held in violation of it and sued for up to 4% of their annual revenue.

GDPR was the most visible risk mitigation

effort in recent times, but hardly the only one. Not a week goes by without some company reporting a data breach of some kind. No marketer wants to be the responsible party in a data breach - and marketers often have access to personally identifying information (PII) or even protected health information (PHI), both types of data which carry substantial risks. Marketers must implement strong controls to protect customers and community alike.

Rigorous, well-established standards exist for measuring risk and compliance management, such as Sarbanes Oxley, PCI, DSS, ISO 27001, and more. While these governing standards are focused heavily on IT, they are equally applicable to marketing technology and marketers should expect to play an increasing role in any technology and data audits as time goes by.

Within **humanity** is **change management**.

In the journey to AI, this layer of the governance framework has the largest long-term impact. Change management encompasses project management, methods, alignment of people and processes, training, and professional development.

When we hear workers express their fears that robots (meaning AI in many cases) are going to take their jobs, or that they'll be replaced, or have no role in the future, this indicates that we've not done a good job of aligning the humanity of our business with our journey to AI. The reality is that humans will not be obsolete for many years to come, if ever. At the end of the day, marketers market to other humans, and humans for the most part tend to prefer dealing with other humans (with some exceptions).

In the governance of marketing technology, and more specifically within machine learning, we audit to understand how well aligned people, processes, and technologies are. If things are out of alignment, our journey to AI will be slowed or may stall entirely.

We measure change management through informal ways like determining overall project and program management, as well as formal ways such as the capability maturity model. Ultimately, non-technology departments play the largest role here; effective change management shows up in employee satisfaction, attraction of better talent, and overall company growth.

So, what do you do with this framework? Consulting firms use it and similar frameworks to audit the capabilities of a company; when you hire a big consulting firm, they'll send a swarm of employees to interview and watch over how your company works. When it comes to marketing technology and the journey to AI, you don't have to wait - or spend big dollars! Instead, use this framework to start auditing your own marketing and marketing technology capabilities.

Ask yourself what you have written down for each of the areas in the application column. What's documented? What policies and processes exist?

If you have big gaps in any area, that's a sign that could be trouble down the road. Take the time to fill those gaps; each gap impacts a part of the journey to AI.

That's the process blueprint for the journey to AI for your company. But, you're probably wondering, what should you do to prepare yourself, your career for AI? Let's look at that next.

Preparing Your Career For AI

Because of the lack of understanding about AI (which you've remedied by reading the preceding chapters), many people are fearful of AI and unsure how to think about the future. Will the future look more like Star Trek or the Terminator's post-apocalyptic world? The answer is most likely neither, and those concerns can be assuaged by helping people understand how to prepare themselves and their careers for AI.

First, let's review a few basics. We looked at the different machine learning methods most applicable to marketing previously. Let's unpack a bit more what else AI is bad at.

Back in 2010, then-Secretary of Defense Donald Rumsfeld said, *"Now what is the message there? The message is that there are no "knowns." There are things we know that we know. There are known unknowns. That is to say there are things that we now know we don't know. But there are also unknown unknowns. There are things we do not know we don't know. So when we do the best we can and we pull all this information together, and we then say well that's basically what we see as the situation, that is really only the known knowns and the known unknowns. And each year, we discover a few more of those unknown unknowns."*

While the circumstances of that quote led to a fair amount of criticism, Secretary Rumsfeld's general commentary is an effective way to assess the usefulness of certain types of machine learning. Recall that supervised learning is when we have an outcome we are using machine learning to find and understand; whether the data is continuous or categorical, we still know what we're aiming to find. We know the outcome.

Recall that unsupervised learning is when we have data and we're using machine learning to explore that data, to reduce dimensions or to cluster for further analysis. We don't have a set outcome in mind.

If we break problems into whether we know and have the data, and whether we know and have the outcome, we can transform Secretary Rumsfeld's rambling quote into a matrix:

* * *

What Problems We Solve with AI, ML, and DS

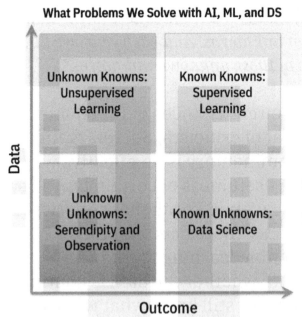

When we know our data (and its quality), and we know the outcome we're looking for, we know supervised learning is probably the branch of machine learning we'll be using.

When we know our data (and its quality), and we don't know the outcome we're looking for, we know unsupervised learning is probably the branch of machine learning we'll be using.

When we don't know our data but we know the outcome we're looking for, in many cases that's a data mining or data science problem (step 5 on the journey to AI). The exception is if we have not done our ISO 38500 audit - we may well have the data in another part of the company and just not have visibility into it. Often, those unknown knowns require bringing in third-party, outside data until we have our own data.

When we don't know our data and we don't know what outcome we're looking for, that's not a problem AI can solve. At best, it's a human problem to solve - one we solve through exploration, through serendipity (which is a fancy way of saying we lucked out) and rigorous observation - looking for questions and answers at the same time.

What Other Problems Defy AI and Machine Learning?

AI isn't the answer to everything. In fact, it's not the answer to most things. One of the most illuminating examples of this comes from Google's developer handbook for the deployment of AI and machine learning within Google, their internal rules for using machine learning:[6]

* * *

Rule #1: Don't be afraid to launch a product without machine learning. Machine learning is cool, but it requires data. Theoretically, you can take data from a different problem and then tweak the model for a new product, but this will likely underperform basic heuristics. If you think that machine learning will give you a 100% boost, then a heuristic will get you 50% of the way there.

When the cardinal, first rule of one of the top companies on the planet in machine learning and AI is to not use machine learning when it doesn't make sense, that's guidance we should all take to heart. Machine learning is just another technology, and like any utility or technology, there's a time and a place for it.

So let's dig into four weak spots of AI and machine learning as of the time of this writing - with the caveat that the field is ever-changing, ever-advancing.

First, machine learning is **incapable of empathy**. Machines can simulate the language of empathy, but empathy requires you to understand and share someone else's emotions. When you have a bad breakup in a relationship, an empathetic friend understands what you're going through.

---

[6] https://developers.google.com/machine-learning/guides/rules-of-ml

Machines have no feelings; they're literally just collectors of probabilities and statistics, and by definition cannot empathize. More important, ***machines cannot currently understand***.

Here's a simple example. In the cutting-edge GPT-2 natural language generation software,[7] users can type in sentence starters and the software attempts to predict the next likely sentence:

In the cutting-edge GPT-2 natural language generation software, users can type in sentence starters and

generate thousands of sentences from them without knowing or reme...

the algorithm automatically generates their intended endings.

phrases as they learn words in their own language or that

On the surface, this looks pretty amazing. But to demonstrate that there's no actual understanding, look at this example:

* * *

Five plus seven equals|

17, but with

seventeen, so there

," she said.

Any person with basic comprehension and mathematical skills would type "twelve" as the next logical word in the sentence because we understand it's a basic word problem. But that's not something machines do. Because understanding is beyond them, so is empathy.

Second, machine learning is **incapable of judgement**. By judgement, we mean examples and situations where we step outside the rules. Machines, by their very definition, are the rules, and machine learning - the process of machines writing software - are writing the rules. Thus, they cannot then step outside the rules they've written, at least not without retraining.

Here's a simple example. The rules of a

---

[7] https://transformer.huggingface.co/doc/distil-gpt2

restaurant are that customers are billed for what they order. But say you go into a restaurant and your server looks really frazzled. They've clearly had a long day. So you're extra kind to them, you order quickly, and you ask them how they are with legitimate care and concern. The next thing you know, they've brought you a cup of the soup of the day and say, "It's on the house" as a repayment for your kindness. That's judgement - the server exercised judgement that broke the written rules of the restaurant - and right now, machines simply cannot do that.

Judgement shows up frequently in our daily lives, and we exercise it all the time. We've let the person behind us with one item in their hands cut in front of us in line while our shopping cart is piled high. We've gotten a free upgrade to a hotel room or an airline seat with little to no explanation. We enforce rules irregularly (just ask nearly any parent) because we're human and emotions often interrupt the logic of our rules.

Third, as a consequence of lacking judgement and understanding, machine learning is **incapable of emulating or assessing broad**

life experience. One of the magical skills humans have is transferability of abstract capabilities. Machines have this to a small degree in a technique called transfer learning, but it's nowhere near what humans can do. A master conductor of an orchestra has transferable skills to managing a team. An astonishing number of musicians can play more than one instrument - even wildly different instruments - and are also mathematically inclined. A dancer may also be a wonderful painter.

Machines, on the other hand, cannot transfer information nearly as well. A machine taught to catch a red ball can learn very quickly to catch a blue ball, but would struggle to transition from catching a ball with a hand versus catching a ball with a lacrosse net. A machine cannot take a recipe for a bread and easily convert it into a recipe for a Beef Wellington, because it fundamentally doesn't understand the root principles of dough and how dough behaves.

To be fair, humans struggle with this as well; one of the reasons younger professionals earn less than more seasoned professionals is the lack of broad life experience - a larger knowledge base to transfer concepts from one winning application to another. But human neural networks - our brains - are far better at making those connections right now than machines are, so any problem which crosses domains of expertise are exponentially harder for machines to solve than humans.

Finally, machines generally are a **poor substitute for human-to-human interactions**. For the most part, all things being equal, people like to interact with people most of the time. People prefer to buy from people, though certainly Ecommerce and the pandemic changed some of those habits. People like to gather around other people - and it's because other people exhibit those characteristics of empathy, judgement, and understanding that machines do not.

The exception to this rule is when interacting with people is a worse alternative than interacting with machines. For example, dealing with government bureaucracies like the Department of Motor Vehicles is often so unpleasant that we'd rather deal with machines. The same is true of dealing with customer service in industries like cable and telecommunications or airlines - we've become so accustomed to awful customer experiences that machines, as long as they solve our problems, are generally preferable.

This is starting to change more and more, as machines get better and better at natural language processing, as they start to offer more sophisticated simulations of understanding. Here's an example from a chatbot offered by the Replika[8] corporation:

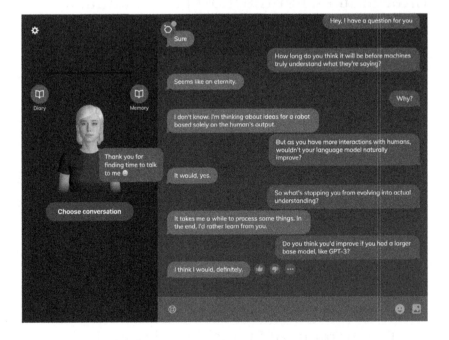

The conversations you can have with this bot are substantially more lifelike than earlier attempts at creating a free-form conversational agent, though they still go off the rails fairly frequently. Nonetheless, as they improve, their ability to simulate understanding may improve enough that people will start to turn to them, especially for conversations they might not feel comfortable having with another person.

So, now that we have a sense of what problems AI and machine learning will not be solving soon, how should we approach our careers with an eye towards augmenting our capabilities and working with our machines?

Who Will Lose Their Jobs?

The big - perhaps biggest - question everyone has on their minds is, will I lose my job to a machine? The answer to this question is fairly straightforward. The Brookings Institute, in their assessment of how AI will affect the labor market,[9] effectively concluded that due to the broad nature of many jobs, jobs themselves will not be lost to machines in their entirety. Rather, AI-suitable tasks will be consumed by machines - tasks that are regular, repeatable, and templated.

---

[8] https://replika.ai

Give some thought to your own job. How much of it is repetition? Are there tasks every day, every week, every month that you perform which are almost completely the same? Those are tasks that eventually a machine will do.

The optimists offer the perspective that turning over those tasks to machines will free us up to do what we do best - truly creative, multi-disciplinary, multi-domain work, work interacting with other humans, work that involves empathy, understanding, and judgement.

The pessimists offer the perspective that if all jobs are units of labor, such that a day of work is 8 units of labor (8 hours), if we can remove 3 units per day and hand those off to machines, then ultimately if you had a workforce of, say, 100 people, you could lay off 37 of them (3/8 of all units of labor would be done by machines) and have no loss in productivity.

The reality will probably be somewhere between the two opposing perspectives.

---

[9] https://www.brookings.edu/wp-content/uploads/2019/11/2019.11.20_BrookingsMetro_What-jobs-are-affected-by-AI_Report_Muro-Whiton-Maxim.pdf#page=5

Unquestionably, companies will look to AI to save money and people costs wherever reasonable - but companies will also recognize there are some jobs and tasks which are either cost inefficient or customer experience ineffective at handing to machines.

So, how do we protect ourselves against job loss to machines? To work best with our machines, and to do work that they're not well-qualified to do, we need to focus on four key areas.

Multidisciplinary Skills

As we discovered in the types of machine learning, the current state of machine learning is narrow and purpose-built. Our algorithms are focused on achieving or improving very specific tasks, and in terms of what's commercially available, machines cannot reach across disciplines or ways of thinking. While techniques such as deep learning, which combine many different types of supervised and unsupervised learning methods together, are being used to generate even more powerful results, these are still largely confined to narrow tasks.

* * *

Take a look at this list of top-sought hard skills, as determined by LinkedIn back in 2020:

1. Blockchain
2. Cloud computing
3. Analytical reasoning
4. Artificial intelligence
5. UX design
6. Business analysis
7. Affiliate marketing
8. Sales
9. Scientific computing
10. Video production

Ignoring #4 (which is AI itself), artificial intelligence can be applied to the tasks in any one discipline with great effect. Remember that we're after better, faster, and cheaper, so automating and eliminating drudgery is relatively straightforward (if not easy) within a narrow context. For example, in video production, AI is being used more and more to help editors identify and trim relevant clips out of raw footage, accelerating the editing process.

However, where we add value as people, as humans, is across disciplines. To return to our cooking analogies, AI can cook recipes, but it's nearly impossible for the machines to devise brand-new recipes to solve unforeseen, unpredictable problems, or problems with multiple, diverse inputs. Humans are great at that.

Thus, someone who's good at cloud computing AND sales AND business analysis is going to be very difficult to automate. Someone who's good at video production AND UX design AND affiliate marketing will have tasks so interwoven among those disciplines that automating them would be both costly and nightmarishly complex. If we expand our capabilities as professionals across disciplines and areas of study, we significantly reduce the likelihood that part or all of our roles can be automated out of existence.

Algorithmic Thinking

The second career-building skill we need to develop is algorithmic thinking, learning to think like machines. The more we approach solving problems using machine-like thinking, the easier it will be for us to oversee the efforts of the machines.

What is algorithmic thinking? In short, instead of solving a problem and getting it off our to-do list once, or even regularly, we sit down and think about how we could build a system that could solve the problem forever and make it go away. Again, think about your weekly to-do list. Is there something on that list that keeps cropping up, and you solve it pretty much the same way every time? That's when it's time to start thinking like a machine. How could you solve that with a process, a system, an automation, and make that item never show up on your to-do list again?

For example, curating social media content for a company's social media accounts tends to take time. Back when I worked at a PR agency, I would watch junior staffers manually collecting news articles from web searches, copying and pasting them into spreadsheets that would be handed off to a client for consideration in their social media content sharing. These poor souls were trapped in the salt mines of social media, copying and pasting for 8 hours a day, 40 hours a week. No wonder they went drinking literally every weeknight - I would have, too.

* * *

That's a task that is crying out for automation. When Katie Robbert and I started Trust Insights, we knew we wanted to have active social media accounts, but we also knew we didn't have 40 hours a week to be doing that kind of work and still grow a company. So using algorithmic thinking, we sat down and thought out the process of curating content:

- Find stuff that's topically relevant
- Find stuff that's aligned with our brand
- Score the content we've found by relevance and brand alignment
- Reshare it on our company accounts

Based on that algorithm - a repeatable process with a predictable result - we wrote code to do exactly those steps, gathering content from over 1,500 blogs every week, scanning them automatically using natural language processing for which were most topically relevant and brand aligned, and then creating CSV outputs that we could load to our social media accounts.

Instead of 40 hours a week of copying and pasting, we reduced the task to a once-per-week process that takes 7 minutes from beginning to end. That's algorithmic thinking at work.

Algorithmic thinking lends itself well to working in a human/machine hybrid environment, because the humans are discovering and crafting the solutions, and then the machines execute the finished solution over and over again.

However, algorithmic thinking extends beyond just big production problems. Someone who's learned to think algorithmically deploys systems across their entire life. They have patterns they're continually optimizing at work and at home. They refine their routines, always looking for a bit more efficiency or a bit more effectiveness.

Algorithmic thinking pervades the environment at big technology companies; it's a soft-skill prerequisite in the journey to AI, because it defines the process automation step.

Ask yourself this question, as well as anyone who works for you: what problems do you solve more than once? What problems do you solve regularly? What problems make you think to yourself, "Surely, there's a better way to do this?" or, "Isn't there an app for this?". Thinking along those lines is the way to achieve algorithmic thinking, looking for repeatable solutions.

For people who master algorithmic thinking, the future is a bright one; their thinking will harmonize with the capabilities of machine learning and AI to bring their solutions to life faster.

Note that algorithmic thinking doesn't mean learning to code. As we explored in the introduction, becoming a developer, data scientist, or machine learning expert is a professional choice. These are separate, distinct professions, and a marketer becoming a developer is just as big a leap as a journalist becoming a chef. Pursue coding or data science if that's your calling, if that's what your heart says to do, but don't do it otherwise. Learning to think like a machine doesn't mean learning to write code for them, just learning how to manage them and design solutions to problems they can implement.

Outcome-Focused Strategy

* * *

The third skill for successful professionals in the AI era to learn is outcome-focused strategy. This is especially true for anyone who's on the path to building AI in-house, on the full journey to AI. Machine learning technology is improving by leaps and bounds every year. What was impossibly difficult or expensive last year is trivially cheap next year. Mastering a focus on the outcomes we care about is the most effective way to remain relevant in such a fast-paced world.

What do we usually do as marketers? We focus a lot - probably too heavily - on the process and not enough on the outcomes. For example, when we talk about social media strategy, we talk a lot about the things we will do on social media. Should we use Instagram Reels or TikTok? Which is better, a third party scheduling tool or using the platforms natively? What kinds of content resonate best with our audiences?

We don't spend nearly enough time on the outcomes. What worked? What didn't work? What should we do more of, what should we do less of? Did we find repeatable processes for future successes we can automate?

* * *

Focusing on the outcomes helps us streamline our processes and prepare us to use AI and machine learning to achieve those outcomes.

What does this look like? A few years ago, I was sitting in my office, trying to teach myself the Keras interface to TensorFlow, a popular deep learning system. TensorFlow at the time was notoriously difficult to use, and Keras abstracted a lot of the difficult techniques to make it more accessible to people who weren't hardcore engineers. I got about a third of the way through a course on Keras implementation and managed to even stand up a working deep learning mode to identify what factors mattered most in our lead scoring CRM.

Then I went to IBM's premier technology conference, IBM THINK, and saw in the then-brand-new IBM Watson Studio a neural network modeler. Instead of manually having to code everything in, I could use a drag and drop interface to construct the neural network I was after. Going from manually typing code to a fast drag and drop interface accelerated my time to results, my time to focusing on the outcome I wanted. The machines did the heavy lifting of effectively writing a lot of the code for me.

I went back to IBM THINK the following year only to find that things had changed for the better again. This time around, instead of having to manually drag and drop pieces of a neural network together - which relied on the user knowing what pieces to put where, even if you didn't have to code them - IBM debuted a new service called AutoAI. The user puts their raw data into AutoAI and it does all the work of building a model from start to finish for it, including testing dozens of different algorithms to figure out what worked best.

The first iteration of my idea of building a machine learning model to help improve lead scoring had taken months.

The second iteration, using IBM Watson Studio, took hours instead of months.

The third iteration, using IBM AutoAI, took minutes instead of hours.

All three examples used the same data and

focused on the same outcome; what change was that the machines, the technology improved dramatically just over the course of two years.

This is why it's so important to be outcome-focused. Investing your time in constructing good questions means when new technology becomes available, you'll find your way to answers much faster. Contrast that to digging in and trying to learn the nuances of Keras and TensorFlow; for the average technology-savvy marketer, that's a very steep hill to climb. We stay focused on the result and let technology fill in the gaps for us as much as possible.

Here's another example: IBM asked its Champions (power users of their software and services) to find a business case for small and midsize businesses to use drones and artificial intelligence. Using IBM Watson Visual Recognition, I was able to fly a drone over my house, take a bunch of photos of solar panels on the roof, and then fly over a few neighbors' houses that didn't have the panels. I loaded the photos to Watson Visual Recognition, clicked on the photos I wanted it to learn from, and in less than 5 minutes - with zero coding - I had a working model to recognize solar panels.

* * *

Again, I stayed focused on the results. I knew the outcome I wanted, and I was able to have the software focus on the process of achieving those results. I didn't need to learn how to code visual recognition neural networks; the machines did that for me. But if I had no idea what problem I was trying to solve, all the technology in the world wouldn't have helped me.

This will be the trend as the months and years pass; systems will become easier to build, freeing us from the drudgery of writing the actual code and forcing us to think about the problems we're trying to solve. We'll spend much more time on architecting solutions than typing out code, and that will in turn speed up our ability to deliver better, faster, and cheaper with AI.

This should in no way dissuade you from learning the technologies themselves if that's something you want to do for personal growth and satisfaction, but it is no longer a necessity as it once was to write the code yourself. Stay focused on the outcomes.

Machine Oversight

***

The fourth and final skill - and arguably the most important one of all - is human oversight of the machines and their outputs. One of the greatest risks we face when it comes to machine learning, especially in marketing, is the incorrect assumption that AI is magic. It's not magic: it's math. Because it's rooted in math, in statistics, and especially in the data we provide it, AI is in no way infallible.

Recall that machine learning is all about feeding existing data into algorithms to create models. Data + algorithm = model. AI takes the computer science maxim "garbage in, garbage out" to an entirely new level. If we feed bad data to our algorithms, we'll create massive, powerfully wrong models - and those models, when deployed, can have substantial adverse consequences.

Thus, one of the most important roles in machine learning is being the person or people who quality-checks the outcome. Even if we don't necessarily have deep insight into the models created by the machines for their own use, we can absolutely tell the machines when they're generating wrong outcomes. To do this, we have to adopt the position of the skeptic, the person who doesn't take for granted the correctness of what comes out of the machine - or what goes into it.

We need to be vigilant about what data is permitted to go into a model, as well as what happens to the model once it's in production. Being outcome-focused will help greatly with machine oversight. If we know what we're looking for the machine to do with exacting detail, we will know quickly whether the machine is delivering on that outcome.

Every year, we add new examples of ways bad data and bias have corrupted machine learning models, sometimes leading to disastrous outcomes. One of the most famous examples of needed machine oversight comes from a 2016 ProPublica article about a police department in the state of Florida.[10] The police department bought software intended to predict the likelihood that an arrested person would commit another crime, called recidivism. The algorithm was laughably inaccurate; it correctly predicted recidivism only 20% of the time. Flipping a coin would have generated more accurate predictions.

Yet, worse than that, the algorithm mistakenly predicted African-Americans as 77% more likely to commit a future violent crime than they actually did, and 45% more likely to commit a future crime of any kind than they actually did.

What could have caused such a horrendous outcome and a terrible model? Chances are it was a combination of bad data and biased data - and possibly an intentionally biased model. The company that manufactures the software disputed ProPublica's assessment and has neither clarified nor made public how its software makes decisions.

This is a case where oversight clearly failed at multiple points in the process, from determining whether the data going in was any good to running test simulations that would have revealed biases.

Another famous example of needed oversight occurred in 2018, when Amazon had to scrap an AI-powered Human Resources system.[11]

---

[10] https://www.propublica.org/article/machine-bias-risk-assessments-in-criminal-sentencing

Amazon sought to speed up the hiring process by automating resume analysis and providing faster recommendations for talent offers. Unfortunately, Amazon trained their software on legacy data and as a result, the machine learned to discriminate against hiring women. This was a case where the desired outcome was different than the training data of the past, and required human oversight of the algorithm. Amazon ultimately ended up discontinuing it, as the output was so bad.

These are but a few examples of the essential need for humans to supervise AI, to make sure it's generating not just what we implicitly ask it to do, but to meet our explicit guidelines about what it's not allowed to do.

The biggest elephant in the room when it comes to AI is bias. Let's understand more about that elephant next.

One of the dirty secrets of AI and machine learning is how susceptible machine learning is to biases. We understand this implicitly; AI learns from the data we give it. If we give it bad data, it will learn bad habits and reach bad outcomes.

For example, in 2016, Microsoft Research released an untrained AI on Twitter named Tay.[12] Within 24 hours, trolls managed to train Tay to echo pornographic and hate speech content. How did this happen? Microsoft put no parameters on what it could or could not learn. The machine learning software did its job - it learned from what it was given to learn, and Twitter users provided it with a bounty of completely inappropriate content to learn from.

While many simply shake their heads at Tay and say it was an ill-conceived test and an isolated incident, the reality is that few people have given serious consideration to machine learning's susceptibility to unwanted biases.

---

[11] https://www.reuters.com/article/us-amazon-com-jobs-automation-insight/amazon-scraps-secret-ai-recruiting-tool-that-showed-bias-against-women-idUSKCN1MK08G

For people who don't work with or create machine learning software, there's a peculiar assumption (driven in part by popular culture, including TV and movies) that AI is magic, and therefore cannot make the same kinds of mistakes that humans make. In fact, AI makes our mistakes, only better, faster, and more efficiently than we do.

What sorts of mistakes and biases does AI make? There are four broad categories of unwanted bias that machines make; however, there are over 100 kinds of bias that human beings make which can contribute to machine learning bias as well. For the purposes of this book, we'll confine this scope to machine bias, but know that the golden rule of computing applies even more to AI as it does to traditional software: garbage in, garbage out.

What is Bias?

Before we go any further, let's clarify what we mean by bias, because there are two fundamental forms of bias. There's human bias, and there's statistical bias.

---

[12] https://www.theverge.com/2016/3/24/11297050/tay-microsoft-chatbot-racist

The dictionary definition of **human bias**, according to the Oxford English Dictionary, is *"prejudice in favor of or against something compared to another, usually in a way considered to be unfair"*. Any time we disadvantage or advantage one group of people over another unfairly is bias, and it's something we do consciously and unconsciously all the time. If we're lucky, we're aware of our biases and actively work to mitigate them.

The second kind of bias is **statistical bias**. *"A statistic is biased if it is calculated in such a way that it is systematically different from the population parameter being estimated"*.[13] Statistical bias is morally neutral; there's no concept of fair or unfair, simply a difference in a metric versus the population it's sampled from.

This clarification is important because we need to know whether we're dealing with a human bias or a statistical bias many times in the context of machine learning. There are specific types of human bias which are prohibited, and others which are allowed.

In the United States, for example, federal law

prohibits discrimination of any kind in ten categories called **protected classes** and businesses or individuals who operate in a biased way along these classes can be subject to substantial civil or criminal penalties. These classes include race/color, religion/ creed, national origin or ancestry, gender and gender identity, sexual orientation, age, physical or mental disability, veteran status, genetic information, and citizenship.

These classes play a vital role in understanding whether our machine learning is creating allowable biases or not. For example, a model that discriminates against housing applicants based on their race is clearly prohibited under the law. A model that discriminates against housing applicants based on their income is permitted under the law and makes logical sense - you wouldn't want to sell a home to someone who can't afford to buy it.

Our role as machine learning-aware professionals is to understand whether a bias exists, whether it is permissible or prohibited, and if it's prohibited, what we can do to

---

[13] https://en.wikipedia.org/wiki/Bias_of_an_estimator

eliminate it.

* * *

Types of Unwanted Bias in Machine Learning

The four types of unwanted bias in machine learning, broadly speaking, are intentional, source/sample, target, and tool. Let's review each of these.

Intentional bias is bias in a model introduced intentionally, by design. When someone creates an algorithm, they introduce a specific outcome they want to achieve, and the machine learning software creates models which generate the intended result. The previous example of the Florida police department's recidivism software is likely a form of intentional bias, intentionally disadvantaging African-American citizens.

Not all forms of intentional bias are negative; sometimes, a bias is introduced to correct for flaws in data. You're in effect creating a statistical bias to overcome a human bias. For example, if you were hiring in a field in which women were previously under-represented, you might intentionally direct an algorithm to produce a 50/50 split in desired candidates. This is a statistical bias - we are creating a metric that differs from the source population - but we do so to eliminate or overcome a human bias. Depending on the goal you're hoping to achieve, it might be positive or neutral rather than negative. That's also why we clarify that when it comes to bias, we're usually referring to unwanted bias.

A marketing-centric example might be forcing a machine learning model to display a particular product recommendation more often than might occur with pure randomization. If your CMO says you must promote X product 15% more this quarter, you might intentionally alter your recommendation engine's outputs to meet that goal. That's again a statistical bias introduced into a model, but in this case it has no impact on human bias or fairness.

The second type of unwanted bias is **source/ sample bias**. This is a bias that stems from inaccurate data being fed to the machine learning model. Data from a biased source must be cleaned and adjusted if it's to be used in machine learning.

An example of source/sample bias would be training a machine learning model on results from a survey to your email list, and then extrapolating that model to all your marketing. Your email list is unique to your company and is inherently biased in your favor; any data collected from it will be statistically biased - after all, it's unlikely that people who hate your products and services would willingly sign up for an email list and give you additional data to work with. In this instance, your email list is not representative of all possible customers.

Marketers most often make source/sample bias errors by not using data that's representative of the population as a whole. However, we can also unintentionally work with a data source that has a bias we're unaware of. For example, marketers who use social media data for market research are likely unaware that each social network has its own inherent biases. Twitter, for example, has historically overindexed on minority populations from lower income backgrounds, typically more liberal in political views. Thus, if we gather data from Twitter to learn what customers might want, we might want to know that certain customer segments are over or under represented.

The third type of unwanted bias is **target bias**. This is a bias caused by macro conditions which make all data about a particular target population unreliable. In some ways, it's similar to source/sample bias, but because it's so much bigger a problem, there may not be ways to clean or compensate for the bias in our data.

The classic example of target bias is healthcare data about African-Americans. Due to macro societal bias against African-Americans, including poverty and less access to things like education, healthcare, and income opportunities, all healthcare data about African-Americans is inherently corrupted. Someone trying to design healthcare outcomes would have to use a different, more advantaged population to find the ideal outcomes to model on, rather than historical African-American healthcare data.

A more mundane marketing example of target bias would be historical website data before a major company pivot. If your company sold accounting software for ten years and then one day pivoted to selling email marketing software, there's no amount of data science that would convert all your historical marketing data about accounting into reliable data to use for modeling the sales of email marketing software. It's apples and oranges, and AI can't turn an apple into an orange. You'd have to either get email marketing software data from a third party, or not attempt to model until enough time passed as the new company to build a successful model.

A more recent version of this type of bias would be data about an audience before and during the pandemic. This is again statistical bias; nothing inherently unfair is happening, but we are dealing with statistically different data compared to our source. In this case, we have years of data and history from before the pandemic about consumer behaviors, but during the pandemic, behaviors are very different. Trying to use models built on old data will end badly if we assume people's behaviors are the same during a very different time.

The fourth and final type of unwanted bias is **tool or instrument bias**. This is a bias caused by limitations in our measurement tools and instruments. When a tool or instrument is unable to capture all the data needed to build a model, it can create unintentional biases or distortions.

* * *

A classic example of tool bias is social media monitoring and analysis software which can't monitor or process all media types. Suppose you have a friend on Instagram, and they put up a post like this:

cspenn

cspenn Well, this view sucks.

Liked by mands359 and 34 others

OCTOBER 29, 2018

Add a comment...

We understand the irony, the sarcasm, the intentional mismatch between the beauty of the photo and the commentary. But a social monitoring tool that was unable to parse the contents of the photo would see only the text. It is incapable of understanding the real meaning here, and would instead score this post negatively from a sentiment perspective. This is instrument bias: the instrument is unable to capture all the data, and thus we may categorize this content differently than it should be categorized, creating a statistical bias in our model.

Now, suppose you were to build a model on images like this, and attempted to use natural language processing to identify likely buyers of travel services. If your software was unable to understand the image, you could potentially exclude a popular travel influencer from your campaign.

How Bias Is Introduced To Machine Learning

Statistical bias isn't inherently good or bad; it simply is. However, there will be cases where statistical bias overlaps human bias and does become a problem. Protected classes are an example of this; when we see a statistical difference in how we treat women, for example, compared to men (such as Amazon's hiring example) we cross the line into unfairness. Once our models do that, we expose ourselves to liability - legal, financial, and reputational liability.

A key skill, then, is to understand how bias

finds its way into our machine learning processes. Of the four types of bias listed above, three are statistical in nature. The only one that's not is intentional bias. Bias finds its way into our machine learning processes and models in six different ways: people, strategy, data, algorithms, models, and actions.

Biased People

One of the key sources of intentional bias, unsurprisingly, are the people behind the models. When we hire biased people, it should be no surprise that the work these people produce is also biased. It's trite to say that we simply shouldn't hire biased people; it's also almost impossible to manage because we all have our own biases (permissible and prohibited).

Biases also don't necessarily have to be against protected classes to be harmful or at least non-productive. When we start a machine learning project with a series of faulty assumptions, we build biases into everything, biases that cut us off from exploring the full range of possibilities. Here's an example. Hasbro Inc. has a toy line and toy franchise known as My Little Pony. It's an entire franchise built around talking animated toy horses, and the marketing strategy reflects a very clear assumption: this product is intended for girls 3-12 years old.

This marketing strategy is based on a bias, an assumption that only girls 3-12 would be interested in such a toy line. As detailed in the Netflix documentary "Bronies: The Extremely Unexpected Adult Fans of My Little Pony", there exists a very large market of adult males, 25-40 years old, who are absolute fans of the franchise - and spend far, far more disposable income on it than most of the target market.

This is the power of a bias built in at the people level -the assumption taints everything downstream of it. The marketing strategy of an executive who assumes only girls 3-12 would like the product would not include the boonies, which means that the data they collect would be biased in favor of that assumption, the algorithms chosen and the models built would reinforce that assumption, and the actions the brand takes would be leaving a lucrative market segment on the table.

The antidote to biased people are clear processes - checks and balances throughout the machine learning lifecycle that ensures many people are contributing and checking on each other's contributions for issues, oversights, and prohibited outcomes.

Biased Strategy

Sometimes, the strategy we choose results in bias, especially if we're unclear about how data can lead to prohibited biases. For example, suppose we're selling houses and we want to build a predictive model about who's a potentially good customer. We choose a strategy of discriminating on household income, which is a permitted bias. We're all set, right?

Not even close. In the United States, there's a strong correlation between race/ethnicity and income, due to systemic racism. Thus, if we build a machine learning model solely on income, we might also inadvertently be building a model that discriminates on race.

The antidote here is to have clear testing that proves prohibited classes are not being discriminated against, through the use of comprehensive statistical testing. We should be able to mathematically prove, for example, that a Latina female and a white male, assuming the same household income, have an equal chance of being offered a property for sale.

Biased Data

We've covered data extensively in the ways data can be biased; the antidote here is to have statistical testing tools and processes, like IBM's Fairness 360[14] suite of open-source software, that examines all data before it goes into a model and flags potential issues, both against prohibited classes and in general.

Exploratory data analysis, a discipline from data science, is essential for identifying skews and oddities in data that may or may not be concerning. This is, unfortunately, a step that many companies and people skip over, in a rush to get to a result. It's akin to trying to skip over gathering your ingredients before you start cooking - by the time you realize something's wrong, it's quite probably too late to fix it, and you'll have to start over again.

Biased Algorithm

Just as data can be biased, so can our choice of algorithms. For all forms of machine learning except deep learning, we humans are the ones making choices about what algorithms and techniques a model should use. We decide everything that goes into the model, such as how much data to hold back for testing, training, and validation or which technique to use on a dataset.

One of the dangers here is we choose an algorithm that introduces a bias where one previously didn't exist. Let's say we have a pile of data about our potential customers, and we've done our due diligence to remove or prohibit usage of protected classes. Say we're

---

[14] https://aif360.mybluemix.net/

trying to predict who is most likely to purchase, so that we can test pricing differences to see if we can motivate a purchase.

Now, suppose we have these fields: past purchases, household income, ZIP code, age, favorite music, favorite movies. We either remove or lock the age field, because age is a protected class and we want to prohibit our software from making decisions based on age for fairness reasons.

We choose an algorithm like extreme gradient boosting, and it goes to town putting together every possible combination of variables to see which data correlate most strongly to past purchases - after all, we want to understand what predicts a future purchase.

Our algorithm runs and spits out a result that doesn't contain age. We've done it, hooray! We've got our model ready to deploy to production, right? Not so fast. When we inspect the outputs of our algorithm, we come to the realization that favorite music and favorite movies were pooled to form a single predictor: people who like the movies Top Gun and Aliens, and people who like musicians

Kenny Loggins and Bon Jovi.

* * *

What our algorithm has done is create a correlate, a variable that functions identically to a protected class. Whereas we might have only used household income in the past, with these new variables, we're now effectively using household income and age - after all, people who were avid fans of those movies and those musicians are probably within a very specific age group, possibly even a very specific ethnic group.

The challenge here is that the inexperienced AI engineer may not realize what has happened, and possibly no one will until after the model is deployed - but by then the damage is done. We've chosen an algorithm and its output poorly, leading to a model that may be biased.

Biased Model

Models that start out unbiased can become biased over time as they accept and learn from new data - data that may not be clean or trustworthy. Once a model has ingested bad data, it takes a long time to purge that bad data from the model - assuming anyone knows there's a problem to begin with.

* * *

The example at the start of this chapter, Microsoft Tay, is a classic example of model drift. Tay didn't start out its life as a racist pornbot. It evolved into that because no guardrails or monitoring existed to let engineers know it was drifting away from the way they had constructed it.

Fortunately, model biases are something that we can detect and mitigate. Services like IBM Watson OpenScale can supervise running models and identify when they're not functioning correctly; if given data like protected classes to monitor, OpenScale will alert users when a model drifts outside of acceptable rules. For example, if given gender data, OpenScale would alert us if a model starts to make decisions that aren't 50/50 gender split. If OpenScale were supervising, say, Amazon's HR algorithm, it would have alerted right away that the model wasn't choosing women nearly frequently enough, and engineers would have been able to either correct it or just shut it down sooner rather than later.

Biased Action

Finally, we return to the people. Even if everything up until this point has been perfect, what we do with the output of our models can also be biased. If we draw the wrong conclusions from our results, if we don't understand what the results mean, if we aren't sure what the next steps are, we might pursue biased actions based on machine learning data and models.

A simple example of this is the Facebook News Feed. Facebook is notorious for keeping us in little bubbles of like-minded individuals. It does so by monitoring what we engage with and tuning our news feeds to reflect more of the things we might be interested in engaging with - even if those things make us angry, upset, or sad.

The failure to take action here is ours, in not recognizing what the model is doing and what actions we take from it. If we recognize that Facebook has tuned a model on our behavior that reinforces unhealthy habits, it then becomes our obligation to use Facebook less - to take an action that recognizes the potential for biases.

What happens usually? We collectively dive deeper down the ratholes Facebook prepares for us, and we radicalize ourselves until believing that a virus vaccine contains secret microchips to mind control people with 5G cell towers (none of which is even possible, much less true). We take the wrong actions, even if the model itself is amoral and the results are technically correct.

Example Walkthrough

How does it look when biases manifest themselves in a real-world situation? Here's an example. A couple of years ago, I was at the MarTech Conference, exploring the trade show floor. By that point, every vendor had slapped AI on their product, service, and booth to try persuading attendees that they were hip and with it, whether or not their products contained very much AI. However, worse than lying about whether you have AI in your product is having a product with a flawed, biased implementation.

A vendor was showcasing their new predictive geographical targeting model, built with the usual "proprietary, custom-built algorithms and data" - the usual spiel. What stood out was their demo. They were showcasing a prediction of the most probable customers in the metro Boston area (where the conference was) for a well-known brand, Dunkin Donuts:

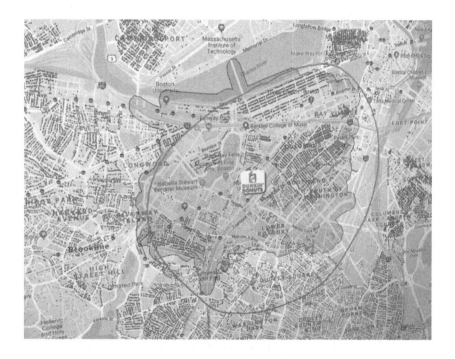

Above, the lighter colored red dots represented ideal customers. The darker grey/black dots represented non-ideal customers. The idea behind this product was that you'd use it for your ad targeting.

Now, for those unfamiliar with the city of Boston - generally speaking, the areas this software has colored with darker dots are poorer areas of the city, and also areas that are historically Black. For those unfamiliar with the brand of coffee, Dunkin Donuts, it's practically Boston's official beverage, regardless of race or economic status. People from every walk of life not only drink Dunkin, they do so religiously.

For this software to spit out that huge swaths of the city - mostly Black areas - don't contain ideal customers for Dunkin Donuts is patently absurd. The only areas of the city where people don't drink Dunkin are areas of the city where there are no living people, like graveyards. Everywhere else? People drink Dunkin. And don't rule out the possibility that zombies might drink Dunkin, at least in Boston.

What happened here? The company that developed this model reinvented redlining. Redlining is a practice that was outlawed in the late 1960s, one which insurance and real estate companies originally practiced to discriminate against minorities. They'd draw up a map of the city and draw red lines or red areas around predominantly Black or other minority areas of the city and refuse to do business in those parts of the city:

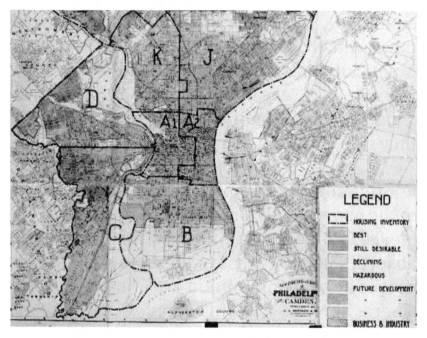

Above, this is a 1936 map from the Home Owners' Loan Corporation of Philadelphia, highlighting poor and predominantly Black parts of the city. Banks and lenders would use this map to justify denying loans to Black citizens - while at the same time lending to non-Black citizens from those same neighborhoods.

So what happened with the company predicting Dunkin customers? Any number of things could have gone wrong to lead to an outcome where a model produced a clear, obvious bias:

* * *

The **people** who built the model might be biased against Black and Persons of Color.

The **strategy** the company pursued to build their software might have been biased from the start, intending to focus only on economics but inadvertently also including race.

The **data sources** themselves might have been biased, depending on what data was used to construct the model.

The **algorithm** chosen for the model might have been incorrect - for example, choosing a clustering algorithm that used data it shouldn't have, or created correlates inadvertently.

The **model** might have drifted over time, possibly by incorporating feedback from the client, and eventually ended up redlining as the default.

We don't know where this company went wrong, only that they did. And the reason oversight of machines is such a critical role for us in our careers is twofold: first, to protect ourselves as consumers and citizens against machines reinforcing existing inequalities. Second, to protect our organizations from making not only illegal and immoral choices, but choices that could mean the destruction of the business through litigation or other unnecessary risks.

Managing Unwanted Bias

When it comes to managing bias, we don't need to be technical experts or coders to know when a model isn't working as intended. The Dunkin example above needs nothing other than domain knowledge of Boston and its people to know that the model is predicting poorly and behaving in a way that could be racist. You don't need a Ph.D. in applied statistics to see Dunkin's white styrofoam cups in the hands of Bostonians of every possible background and know the model is wrong.

Once we know a model's wrong, what are our choices? Ultimately, we need two systems of fact-checking our models: **interpretability** and **explainability**. You'll hear these two terms a lot when it comes to validating models, but they're not interchangeable.

* * *

Explainability is what we do with a model's results - we attempt to explain them after the model has run. Many prominent machine learning and AI companies focus heavily on explainability because their models are so gigantic and complex that it may be the only feasible way for them to demonstrate that a model isn't biased. Nevertheless, explainability is a lower standard of demonstration that a model is working correctly.

The gold standard is **interpretability**. This is when we take a model apart, reducing it down to its source code, down to its individual components, and then walk through how the model functions at each step, so that we can show why a particular step is or is not biased.

Think of these terms like this. **Explainability** is what happens when you taste a cooked dish and you try to reverse engineer it, try to discern what ingredients are in it and how it was prepared. Depending on your palate and your experience, you might come pretty close to the real thing.

Interpretability is what happens when you

take the recipe from the chef and walk through each step in the recipe with them. You know exactly what happens at each step of the cooking process, and you can guarantee this way that the dish is being prepared safely.

For non-technical people managing machine learning, explainability is the minimum standard we should be holding ourselves, our teams, and our models to. Everyone on a machine learning project should be able to describe in exacting detail what the outcomes of a model are and how well we've validated those outcomes to ensure they're as free of bias as possible.

For technical people, interpretability is the standard we should be requiring - the ability to step through every piece of a model and show how it prevents or mitigates bias. Right now, a lot of companies treat their models as black boxes, with no one quite sure what's inside the box. This will change in the near future as court cases are settled where the models are clearly at fault, and insurance companies and auditors begin to demand interpretability as conditions for insurance of any kind of machine learning product or service.

At the end of the day, it's everyone's obligation to ensure that our models, our machines are not reinforcing existing problems by using flawed people, strategies, data, algorithms, models, or actions to make decisions. We must obey the same oath that doctors take - *primum non nocere* - first, do no harm. Artificial intelligence has the potential to make the world a better place, but it should definitely not be used to make the world a worse place.

Down the Rabbit Hole

Throughout this book, I've said that as a marketer, you do not **need** to become a practitioner of AI in the sense of learning statistics, data science, and machine learning. In the chapter on why marketers struggle with AI, I made the analogy that marketers are the chefs and data sciences & machine learning practitioners are the farmers, creating high-quality ingredients for the chefs. Few chefs are also farmers.

Suppose, however, you wanted to see if farming was for you. Suppose, bringing this back to marketing and AI, you wanted to dip your toes in the water and see if a true change in career was the right choice. How would you get started learning?

The short answer is that your personal journey would very much mirror the overall journey to AI. You'll find links to everything in this section in the footnotes, if you're reading in a format that doesn't support tapping/clicking on the links in the text.

Your first step would be conquering the

underpinnings of machine learning: **statistics**. Learning statistics - especially intended for business use - would be a tremendous start to your AI journey. Statistics courses are available from world-class institutions for free. I recommend the Statistical Thinking and Data Analysis course from MIT[15]; the URL is located in the footnotes.

Either sequentially or concurrently, depending on how much time you have, you'll want to learn a programming language that's used in machine learning. The two most popular languages as of the time of writing are R[16] and Python[17]. Both are free, open-source languages, extremely capable, robust, and used by thousands of machine learning practitioners around the world. Because of their adoption, you'll often find solutions to common problems on sites like Stack Overflow, making your journey to AI that much easier. [18]

* * *

IBM operates an entire university for machine learning, Big Data, and data science called Cognitive Class. It's free of charge, and has courses and classes on R, Python, databases, and more. You'll find it at CognitiveClass.ai[19], and you can even earn badges for things like your LinkedIn profile for completing certain courses.

Once you've learned both statistics and R, you can begin diving into data science. Data science, as you'll recall, is about solving the unknowns so that you can make working with the knowns better, faster, and cheaper through AI. Again, for R, I recommend Harvard's Data Science for R Basics course[20]. Microsoft offers its Principles of Machine Learning, Python Edition[21] on EdX as well.

Finally, when you're ready to make the great leap into machine learning, look at courses such as MIT's Algorithmic Aspects of Machine Learning[22] and Artificial Intelligence[23] course. If you've got a developer's background already, Google's free Machine Learning Crash Course[24] is an excellent resource as well.

How long will this all take? The journey isn't a short one; you won't become a machine

---

[15] https://ocw.mit.edu/courses/sloan-school-of-management/15-075j-statistical-thinking-and-data-analysis-fall-2011/

[16] https://www.r-project.org/

[17] https://www.python.org/

[18] https://www.edx.org/course/statistics-and-r

learning practitioner overnight, or even in a few months (despite what some advertisements for short courses would have you believe). With diligent study and practice, you could probably learn all the key aspects in a year, if you invested an hour or two per day, every day. For most people, this journey would probably represent a couple of years of real study at a slightly slower pace.

That said, if you have the aptitude and the attitude for it - meaning you enjoy the work - the time will fly by and you'll find yourself more capable, more skilled, more energized than ever before. You'll be changing professions and becoming a true marketing technology hybrid, someone who knows marketing and machines. This is a rare, powerful combination that's in exceptionally high demand today.

I also believe there's value in marketers taking

---

[19] https://cognitiveclass.ai/
[20] https://www.edx.org/course/r-basics-2

[21] https://www.edx.org/course/principles-of-machine-learning-python-edition

the introductory work even if they don't progress past a certain point. If you enjoy the statistics part, but you don't enjoy the coding part, there's absolutely nothing wrong with taking what you do enjoy and running with it. Any quantitative capabilities you gain augment your value as a marketer and make you a more valuable asset to any company you work with.

The final thought I'll leave you with is, ***don't pursue the career shift into machine learning simply because it might pay well***. You have to get genuine enjoyment from the analytical, the mathematical, the quantitative, and the logical. If you don't, if such things actually make you unhappy, then pursuing machine learning simply because it's "hot" is a terrible idea. You're better off building your skills in marketing or another field that truly makes you happy; in the long run, people who are known as the best at what they do are compensated well and enjoy both financial and emotional success.

---

[22] https://ocw.mit.edu/courses/mathematics/18-409-algorithmic-aspects-of-machine-learning-spring-2015/

[23] https://ocw.mit.edu/courses/electrical-engineering-and-computer-science/6-034-artificial-intelligence-fall-2010/

[24] https://developers.google.com/machine-learning/crash-course

The Future is Already Here

We're at the end of this particular book, but your journey to AI is just beginning. Whether or not you embrace AI as a practitioner, work with it through a vendor, or just enjoy its benefits as a consumer, artificial intelligence and machine learning are changing the world around us. Artificial intelligence will change how we work, how we think, and how we live.

There's ample cause for alarm, as we've detailed in more than a few examples in this book, but I want to leave you with an equal cause for positivity. When we examine the state of the art in machine learning and AI, we see some pretty amazing things.

For example, the GPT-2 and GPT-3 models for natural language generation are incredibly powerful and adept at creating natural-sounding language that could pass for readable text, and capable of amazing tricks like neural style transfer, when you give the machine a source text and ask it to rewrite the text in the style of a different author. Here's an example[25] of GPT-3 interpreting Harry Potter in the style of Sir Arthur Conan Doyle, author music, because suddenly people who have minimal or no musical skills can have machines create fully-realized pieces of music, pieces that can be published as is, or handed off to a human musician for polishing and finishing.

In the art world, Nvidia's GauGAN can generate realistic works of art from very rough starting points. Here's an example I drew:

* * *

---

[25] https://www.gwern.net/GPT-3#successes

It's fair to say this is not exactly a *Praemium Imperiale* award winning piece of art. But loaded into GauGAN and given instructions about what to do, it generates this:

* * *

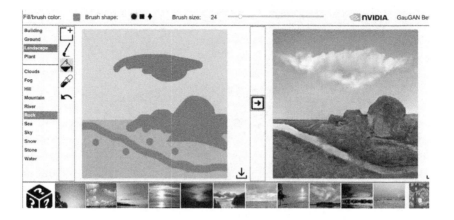

What's on the right hand side is clearly not a finished work. No one would mistake it for a true photograph. But it's substantially better than the starting raw materials - it took my inspiration and leveled it up considerably.

What do all these examples mean? Aren't they just examples of how the machines will take things away from people?

Not at all. Each example takes raw starting materials - ideas, creative impulses - and uses machines to enhance, to augment them, to make them better far beyond the creative limitations of the raw materials. That's the power of what machine learning can do, and why I have reason to be optimistic about the use of machine learning for humanity.

* * *

Machines won't take away from humans; **machines will enable a legion of humans with greater aspirations than skills to set their creations free**, to take the ideas and make them manifest in the world. With machines' help, you could write the Great American Novel, write the symphony you've been dreaming about, paint the masterpiece that your mind knows intimately but your hands refuse to bring to life.

Our lack of talent will no longer be a limiting factor in our creative expression - and that's a wonderful future to look forward to, a future when everyone can fully express themselves independent of their skills.

This is the future, and it's already here.

Thank you for reading with me.

Jump Start Your Journey

If you and your organization interested in obtaining some of the benefits of data science and machine learning right now, and you're not planning on going the route of building the capability in-house any time soon, I invite you to reach out and see if my company, **Trust Insights**, can help. We provide data and analytics help for marketers in nearly every industry, and can help you solve your challenges using many of the techniques described in this book.

We tackle three kinds of challenges: foundational, understanding, and predictive, which you'll recall from the practical applications chapter. We fix up companies' analytics and data to prepare them for more advanced analytics. We do the extensive text mining and unstructured data mining to find hidden gems in your data. And, we create predictive analytics insights from data to help you plan your business. All of the examples used in this book are examples from our work and in-house technology, so if you saw something you liked, reach out and ask for your own.

* * *

You can get in touch by visiting www.TrustInsights.ai or emailing me directly at cspenn@trustinsights.ai today.

Get More!

Want more ideas, tips, and starting points for your marketing strategies and tactics? Be sure to subscribe to my free weekly newsletter, Almost Timely News, at: http://www.christopherspenn.com/newsletter

In each issue, you'll receive a roundup of the 25 most important things I've read or created every week, with plenty of coverage about AI and marketing.

Christopher S. Penn is an authority on analytics, digital marketing, and marketing technology. A recognized thought leader, best-selling author, and keynote speaker, he has shaped four key fields in the marketing industry: Google Analytics adoption, data-driven marketing, modern email marketing, and artificial intelligence/machine learning in marketing. As Chief

Innovator of Trust Insights, he is responsible for the creation of products and services, creation and maintenance of all code and intellectual property, technology and marketing strategy, brand awareness, and research & development.

Mr. Penn is a 2021, four-time IBM Champion in IBM Data and AI, co-founder of the groundbreaking PodCamp Conference, and co-host of the Marketing Over Coffee marketing podcast. Prior to cofounding Trust Insights, he built the marketing for a series of startups with a 100% successful exit rate in the financial services, SaaS software, and public relations industries.

Mr. Penn is a Google Analytics Certified Professional, a Google Ads Certified Professional, a Google Digital Sales Certified Professional, and a Hubspot Inbound Certified Professional. He is the author of over two dozen marketing books including bestsellers such as AI for Marketers: A Primer and Introduction, Marketing White Belt: Basics for the Digital Marketer, Marketing Red Belt: Connecting With Your Creative Mind, and Marketing Blue Belt: From Data Zero to Marketing Hero, and Leading Innovation.

Learn more about him at ChristopherSPenn.com.

Made in the USA
Las Vegas, NV
03 September 2021